"Undeniably, for me 1950 and 1951 were vintage years for courage, valor, and heroism. And, while I associated with the 18th Fighter Group pilots of those old F-51 Mustangs, I can proudly state that I ate with heroes, I drank with heroes, and, to a certain extent, a part of me died with many of those heroes. As a result of my Korean air war experiences, I am firmly convinced that valor and courage are not inborn; they are not hereditary. Instead, they are the result of their then-current environment: When you are surrounded by heroes, it is damned difficult not to perform like one!"

Lieutenant Colonel Duane E. "Bud" Biteman, USAF, Ret.

"A very welcome contribution . . . Chancey and Forstchen have done an outstanding job in taking the 'Forgotten' out of the Forgotten War."

Richmond Times-Dispatch

D0801946

HOT SHOTS

AMERICA'S
FIRST JET ACES

**EDITED BY JENNIE ETHELL CHANCEY
AND WILLIAM R. FORSTCHEN**

HarperTorch
An Imprint of HarperCollins*Publishers*

The photographs in *Hot Shots* are the property of the contributors credited. They are reprinted with permission.

❦

HARPERTORCH
An Imprint of HarperCollins*Publishers*
10 East 53rd Street
New York, New York 10022-5299

Copyright © 2000 by Bill Fawcett and Associates
ISBN: 0-380-81767-5

First HarperTorch paperback printing: June 2002
First William Morrow hardcover printing: April 2000

HarperCollins ®, HarperTorch™, and ❦™ are trademarks of Harper-Collins Publishers Inc.

Printed in the United States of America

Visit HarperTorch on the World Wide Web at www.harpercollins.com

10 9 8 7 6 5 4 3 2 1

CONTENTS

ACKNOWLEDGMENTS

I don't know how to adequately thank all of the Korean War flying veterans who gave me so much for this project. I received numerous letters, phone calls, and E-mails throughout my work on the book, all of which encouraged me and helped me in some vital way. A very special thank-you must go to my grandfather, Col. Ervin C. Ethell, who served with the Korean Military Advisory Group during the conflict. He was a great source of information on this "Forgotten War" and supplied me with my first list of contacts. Col. "Pancho" Pasqualicchio was also a tremendous help to me, giving me names of pilots to contact for interviews and steering me in the right direction from the start. He also had some fabulous stories to tell. Col. Gerald Brown of the American Fighter Aces Association pulled out all the stops to get me in touch with Korean War aces and made it easy to introduce myself and this project to them. Without Col. Duane "Bud" Biteman, I never would have found one tenth of the history of the 18th Fighter-Bomber Wing, nor would I have been able to get in touch with so many fantastic veterans of that group. Col. Biteman' s own web-site was an invaluable resource, and his generous offer of his own recollections and color slides gave me a great amount of material. Gratitude must also be expressed to those men who took the time to talk on the phone with me or correspond in detail about their missions in Korea: Lt. Gen. Frederick "Boots" Blesse, Col. Harold Fischer, Col. Cecil Foster, Col. William Gunter, Maj. James Kiser, Lt. Col. Raymond MeKelvey, Col. Bill Myers, Col. Ralph Parr, Brig. Gen. Robinson Risner, and Col. Ralph "Salty" Saltsman. I am also thankful to the many veterans who took time to write and send articles or other personal information even when they were not able to participate in interviews: Lt. Col. John F. Bolt, Maj. James Brooks, Larry Davis of *Sabrejet Classics*, Denis Earp of the South African Air Force, Maj. Jim Low, Col. Walker "Bud" Mahurin, Lt. Gen. W.W. "Bones" Marshall, Col. Harry Moreland, Dolph Overton, Brig. Gen. Lon Walter, and Lt. Col. William Wescott. Your contributions were greatly appreciated. I wish I could have spoken with every flying vet who contributed so much to the Korean effort—we owe you so much.

Thank you to my husband, Matt, who patiently listened to my excited chatter over MiG Alley missions, life in the "Dog Patch," and daring behind-the-lines rescues. It sure is nice to be married to another history nut!

And, finally, a great thank-you must go to my late father, Jeffrey L. Ethell, who was my mentor, writing teacher, chief inspiration, and dearest comrade. If I hadn't spent three summers working as his research assistant and hadn't grown up immersed in Warbirds, fighter pilots, and air shows, my participation in this project would never have been a reality. It's hard to take even a couple of steps in your boots, Dad, but I'm honored to have walked in them for a short while.

Jennie Chancey

ABOUT THE PHOTOGRAPHS

The photographs appearing in *Hot Shots* were taken by U.S. Air Force combat pilots and their contemporaries. They are meant to illustrate some of the overall military activities occurring during the oral histories related in these pages. They are not meant as literal illustrations of the specific stories in this book.

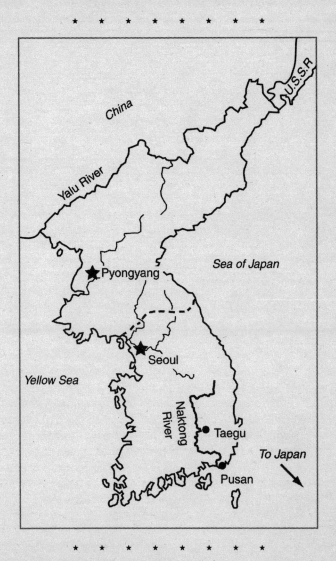

KOREA 1950

China

U.S.S.R

Yalu River

Pyongyang

Sea of Japan

Yellow Sea

Seoul

Naktong River

Taegu

To Japan

Pusan

HOT SHOTS

1

ORIGINS OF THE WAR

It is known as the "Forgotten War," the conflict on a minuscule peninsula jutting off the eastern flank of the Eurasian landmass. It was the battlefield of former allies, who having turned on each other would use the peninsula of Korea as the testing ground of will and resolve. It was a conflict that would eventually claim the lives of more than 50,000 Americans, hundreds of thousands of Chinese, and more than a million Koreans, North and South.

It was as well the proving grounds of post–World War II aviation technology, for over Korea the first generation of jet aircraft would take to the skies and tangle in deadly combat with closing speeds of over a thousand miles an hour. It was the battlefield of Sabres and MiGs, Hot Shots and Honchos.

It was the home address of MiG Alley, where the professional knights of the Cold War jousted in the icy stratosphere and faced a fiery death.

★ ★ ★

A jet aircraft first flew into harm's way during World War II. On July 25, 1944, a British Mosquito fighter-bomber—a twin-engine propeller aircraft and the fastest airplane in the RAF arsenal—took off from an airfield in England, climbed out to 40,000 feet, and headed into Nazi Germany on a routine reconnaissance flight.

The Mosquito, when stripped down for reconnaissance purposes, was all but invulnerable, capable of soaring far above the highest-reaching flak, and able to outrun anything sent up to catch it. Without weapons, it relied on speed and the ability to climb through 40,000 feet. With supercharger engines and 100-octane a.v. gas in its tanks, nothing could touch it. About the only way one could be brought down was either through the sheer incompetence of the pilot (or his ground servicing crew), or by the lucky placement of a German fighter ahead of the aircraft for a single head-on approach. After that one attack, by the time the German turned around, the Mosquito was already out of range.

With that in mind, the British pilot was undoubtedly amused by the sight of a German fighter climbing up for an intercept from behind. Within seconds of spotting the German fighter though, the British pilot started to worry. The approaching plane was doing the impossible: it was actually climbing up to 40,000 feet and closing in at the same time. The Brit nosed his aircraft over into a shallow power dive, the standard procedure for shaking off pursuit. Usually the biggest worry for a Mosquito pilot at this point was that he might exceed the maximum airspeed of his aircraft. As he approached Mach 1, compression on the trailing edge of the wings would lock his controls until the wings sheared off.

Pushing his aircraft to the limit, he continued the

dive. The German, however, continued to close, swung in on the Mosquito's tail, and fired off a burst before streaking overhead. He had come in so fast that he had not had time to line up his shot properly. The British pilot watched in amazement as the German pulled into a tight banking turn, rolled out, and lined up for a second pass.

Thoroughly shaken by this close encounter of the worst kind, the unarmed British pilot sweated out a frightening twenty-minute game of cat and mouse, pitting skill against raw power until the hunted finally managed to gain a high, rolling bank of cumulus clouds.

After hiding in the mists for several minutes, the British pilot slipped back out into the open. The mystery plane was gone. Turning west, he raced back for England, bearing a report about a Nazi fighter with a sharklike fuselage . . . the first combat encounter involving a jet aircraft had come out a draw.

Much has been written about this remarkable new superweapon, the German ME-262. Under development since before the start of the Second World War, it might very well have premiered a full year earlier, but development was hampered by miscalculations, misdirection of resources, and outright stupidity as to its proper tactical application. Delay after delay crippled development because of Hitler's insistence that the new jet be used for ground attack rather than placed in the realm where it belonged, as a weapon for air superiority over Germany.

When it did reach the skies over Germany, it was a matter of too little, too late. Less than a thousand 262s ever took to the air, and the Allies finally mastered the technique for dealing with both this plane and the tiny ME-163 rocket glider, a suicidal machine that was little more than a rocket with a pilot strapped to the front of it.

In straight-up head-to-head combat, no Allied plane could hope to match the 262 in terms of speed. Its firepower was frightfully deadly, packing four 20-millimeter cannons aligned on the fuselage compared with the standard American arrangement of six .50-caliber, wing-mounted machine guns on the P-51 and P-47.

Its point of vulnerability, however, was on the ground or in the first and last few minutes of flight. The 262 was slow to accelerate and if caught in a takeoff or landing pattern, it was a target even a novice could hit.

The ME-163, within seconds after takeoff, could accelerate up to 500 mph, but it carried fuel for less than ten minutes of powered flight. Within seconds after takeoff, the 163 pointed up into a 70-degree climb and in less than two minutes was at 25,000 feet, where it had enough fuel for eight minutes of combat. Once out of fuel, the 163 was nothing more than a high-speed glider, falling back to its base for a powerless landing.

American and British tactics evolved out to tracking the new jet or rocket planes to their bases and pouncing on them as they landed, or were already down. The Germans countered with attempts to maintain patrols of older prop planes to escort the jets and rocket planes in, but sheer numbers usually overwhelmed this tactic, and every fighter jock in the USAAF and RAF wanted the boasting rights that they had dropped a jet. Whenever a 262 or 163 showed up it was certain to attract a swarm of fighters in reply.

In addition, the German jet program was hampered by a crisis in pilot training and logistical support. By 1944, training had been cut back to the point where novice pilots were often going into combat with less than a hundred hours of air time, making them live bait for Americans and Brits with upwards of five hundred hours of training. Many 262 pilots were given but one familiarization flight with the new jet before being sent into action.

Finding a safe spot for training was all but impossible by late 1944, with dawn-to-dusk patrols sweeping across Germany. And, finally, the complex task of keeping the air bases supplied with fuel and spare parts was nearly impossible under the incessant pounding from above. More and more 262s were simply destroyed on the ground (in fact, this is where a majority of them were wiped out), targets waiting to get hit because they lacked an engine, hydraulic fluid, or fuel.

The new wonder weapons of Hitler were, fortunately, too little, too late. A thousand 262s massed and waiting in 1943 might very well have changed the course of the air war. The Germans realized at last their folly in delaying development, and in the final months of the war effort, pushed ahead with a wide diversity of jet aircraft, such as the "people's fighter," the HE-162, a single-engine plane designed for cheap mass production; the Gotha (or Horten) 229 flying wing; and a lightweight sweep-wing design intended for supersonic flight.

As the victorious Allies swept into Germany, the race was on to feast on the technological corpse of the Nazi empire. Even before the 262 took to the skies, Britain, America, and the Soviet Union were all active in the development of jet aircraft. The British Meteor, deployed at about the same time as the ME-262, was but a poor second. Its combat role was limited to operations over England, pursuing V-1 buzz bombs, though a unit was deployed on the continent in the last weeks of the war but never encountered its Nazi rival. The British Meteor pilots hoped for a chance to tangle with the 262s, and thus lay claim to the boasting rights for the first air-to-air jet encounter. However, the war ended before such an encounter could take place. Most likely, this was for the best, since the 262 was a vastly superior aircraft.

America, at the same time, had flown the Bell XP-59, but its performance was even worse, with speeds barely above 400 mph. Russia had yet to get into the air with any viable combat jet aircraft. Thus all three saw Germany as a storehouse of knowledge, practical design, and operational experience when it came to fielding combat-capable jet aircraft.

ME-262s, 163s, Arado 234 four-engine jet bombers, and prototypes of other futuristic aircraft were captured, disassembled, and shipped back to England, the States, and the Soviet Union. Hundreds of technicians, engineers, pilots, and ground crews were taken as well and set to work in labs and airfields (or slave-labor camps), laying the foundation for the forty-five-year arms race in the sky between the East and the West. Korea would be the first testing arena for this new paradigm of air combat.

The impact of German design on all the major powers was soon evident, but it was the Russians who truly startled the world with the premier of the MiG 15 at a Soviet Aviation Day airshow in 1948. Clearly influenced by the swept-back wing of the 262 and other German designs, which were still in the prototype stage at the end of the war, its flight characteristics were boosted far beyond the German design by the use of a British Rolls-Royce turbojet engine, which was inexplicably released by the government for export in 1947.

The MiG 15 was a quantum leap in aircraft design for the Soviets and caught western designers completely off guard, upsetting the assumption that they would most likely maintain a full generational lead over Eastern Bloc aircraft developments. The other major advantage that the Russians had but the West was not yet aware of was one of personnel.

Throughout the four years of the Great Patriotic War, Soviet pilots had fought at a technological disadvantage. By 1943, they increasingly maintained a numerical advantage in the air, but were still hampered by aircraft that usually lacked the technological edge held by the Luftwaffe. Thus pilots learned to wring every ounce of performance out of their aircraft and fought with a mindset that acknowledged the technical superiority of their opponents. This experience and training, when married to a jet that was at the forward edge of design, would prove to be a deadly combination. One of the great misassumptions of the American air force was that Soviet pilots were too rigid in their tactics, lacked the ability to fight independently, and were not technologically oriented enough for jet age combat.

Yet another advantage of Soviet-designed aircraft was the K.I.S.S. principle (keep it simple, stupid). The MiG 15 would prove to be an aircraft of rugged design, capable of absorbing punishment, and able to be turned around quickly by ground crews with limited skills and poor logistical backup. In addition, the MiGs were capable of operating under the most primitive of conditions, while American aircraft increasingly needed clean, paved runways, enclosed hangars, and complex infrastructure for support.

In America a number of significant jet designs took to the air in the immediate postwar years. The first was the Lockheed F-80 Shooting Star, the first combat-capable jet designed by the United States. Learning from the mistakes with the Bell XP-59, Lockheed launched into a full-scale development effort, and in less than half a year came out with the prototype of the Shooting Star. The first combat squadrons were formed early in 1945. F-80s were actually shipped to the Pacific and were slated for introduction in Operation Olympic, the November invasion of Japan, their mission to counter the Japanese Baka, a manned version of the German V-1. The Shooting Star's single Allison turbojet engine delivered a top thrust of 3,850 pounds. Armed with six fuselage-mounted .50-caliber guns, it had weapons points on either wing for multiple rocket launchers or up to 2,000 pounds of bombs.

In spite of the introduction of the F-80 at the very end of the war, the legendary P-51 Mustang continued to serve as the primary American fighter in the immediate postwar years for the simple reason that well over 10,000 of them were still on the government roster.

An interesting variant on the P-51, the F-82 twin Mustang was developed as well. (In the immediate postwar period the United States Air Force changed its fighter designation from "P" for "pursuit" to "F" for "fighter.")

The original P-51 had proven itself as an excellent bomber escort for the armada that had devastated Germany, but it was not until forward bases had been seized at Iwo Jima and Okinawa that it could make the long haul to cover the B-29s over Japan. Having learned the bloody lesson that unescorted bombers would be savaged over any heavily defended target, designers came up with the idea of bolting two P-51s together in a side-by-side arrangement. The shared center wing served as a weapons platform; the outer wings and fuselages as flying gas tanks. The F-82 had an operational radius of over 2,000 miles when fully loaded and could carry two pilots, one in each fuselage, with one of the two serving as co-pilot and weapons officer. Several hundred of this variant were built, with the primary mission to serve as escorts for the superlong-range B-36 bomber.

The United States Navy, at the end of the Second World War, carried on its flight decks one of the most versatile prop fighters of the war, the gull-winged Voight Corsair. Truly one of the great multipurpose aircraft of the war, it could carry a wide diversity of munitions in addition to its six .50-caliber wing-mounted guns and proved its capability in air superiority and tactical ground support, and as a fighter-bomber. The last weeks of the war also saw the deployment of the A-1 Skyraider, an aircraft that would still be in the naval arsenal twenty-five years later during the Vietnam conflict.

The navy's first jet for carrier use was the F9F Panther. Though a prototype had been unveiled at the very end of the war, design problems and budget concerns kept it off the flight deck until 1949. Armed with four 20-millimeter cannons and capable of carrying

2,000 pounds of ordnance, it had a top speed of only 526 mph.

The best of the western air-superiority weapons on the eve of the Korean conflict was a plane originating out of a design competition for the navy, the North American F-86 Sabre, another great jet aircraft. The air force would finally adopt the plane, which incorporated the change from straight wing to sweep, like the MiG 15, a design evolving out of the German ME-262.

Armed with six .50-caliber guns on the fuselage, it delivered a deadly concentrated punch, supplemented by wing-mounted weapons pods that could carry rockets, bombs, or napalm. Capable of reaching speeds bordering on Mach 1, this armored knight was capable of going head-to-head with the MiG 15.

★ ★ ★

The political origins of the Korean conflict can be traced to the Yalta Conference of February 1945. It was at this conference that President Roosevelt received a promise from Stalin that within ninety days after the ending of the war in Europe, Russia, which had maintained neutrality with Japan throughout the conflict, would enter the fight.

The wisdom of pushing Russia to enter the battle has been debated ever since, but in the context of the times, the desire to see Russia in the fight was a logical one. The potential of the Manhattan Project was still an unknown. Though the bitter campaign across the Pacific was proving successful, it had come at a bloody price and with a noticeable increase of fanatical resistance as the ring closed on Japan. In China the war had actually taken a turn for the worse in 1944.

Threatened by the building of B-29 bases on mainland China, the Japanese had launched an offensive with over one million troops, capturing bomber bases that had taken years to build, and sent the Nationalist and American forces reeling.

The nightmare scenario for American planners was that if the United States were forced to invade Japan, hundreds of thousands of Japan's best combat infantry would be transferred from China and Manchuria, with a holocaust for both sides as a result. By getting Russia to commit, Roosevelt hoped for a threefold impact, the first being the tying down and destruction of Japan's reserve of infantry and armor formations on the mainland of Asia; second, the capture of heavy industrial resources in Manchuria; and finally, the striking of a serious psychological blow.

All three effects were achieved when Russia entered the conflict the day after the bombing of Hiroshima. Within a week, in a remarkable and historically neglected campaign, Soviet troops overran nearly all of Manchuria, inflicting hundreds of thousands of casualties on the Japanese. Russian historians have maintained—and there is some validity to their argument—that the Soviet entry into the war, along with the twin bombings of Hiroshima and Nagasaki, were a key factor in the collapse of the Japanese war cabinet and the decision to sue for peace.

Korea, which had been occupied by Japan since the middle of the nineteenth century, was now one of the spoils of war. In the days after the end of the conflict, American occupation troops landed in the south while Russian troops flooded into the north. It was agreed that the 38th parallel, which roughly divided the peninsula in half, would be the line of demarcation for the two occupation forces.

Even at the start, this dividing line was a source of tension, with the Russians declaring that all of Korea should be within their zone of occupation. Soviet interest in Korea dated back to the nineteenth century as well, offering to the Soviet navy the potential of several year-round ports. It jutted like a finger straight at Japan and also provided a strategic flank to the coast of northern China. The Russians sealed off their half of the zone and worked to form a puppet state.

By 1949, the paradigm for the future conflict was in place. The Cold War had nearly gone hot the year before in Berlin, Russia had successfully detonated its own atomic weapon, and in that same year Maoist forces had expelled the last of the Nationalists, declaring China a Communist state.

The geopolitical situation was now a tense one. Russia, China, and Korea had been rivals throughout most of history. Korea in its own right had once been noted as a significant military power, relying on the harsh mountainous region of the north and its tough peasantry for defense. Korea had repeatedly defeated Chinese expansionist forces throughout the Middle Ages and had dealt a devastating defeat to the Japanese in the early 1600s. They had resisted as well Russian expansionist efforts in the eighteenth and early nineteenth centuries before succumbing to the Japanese. Prior to the advent of communism, China and Russia could have been expected to make sure that neither side gained a true hegemony on the peninsula. This was now changed with Mao still dependent on the Soviet Union for military and technical support; thus Chinese and Russian foreign policy regarding a united and Communist Korea came together.

Taken from the Communist perspective, Korea was

the only mainland base available to America that could threaten both China and the Soviet Pacific base at Vladivostok. Therefore, for both the Communist and free world forces, Korea was a potential platform for offensive operations, while at the same time a significant threat if controlled by the enemy.

In spite of these concerns, American troops started to withdraw from Korea in 1949. Combined with this was a confused foreign policy signal, not unlike a later situation in Kuwait, where the other side was allowed to work under the misassumption that U.S. strategic concerns for Korea were minimal and a serious commitment to defense against aggression was unlikely.

The armed forces of North Korea, over 90,000 strong, were well equipped, including a significant armor force of the superb Russian T-34 tank. In contrast, the forces of South Korea were equipped by their American sponsors with only light weapons, and no heavy antitank equipment. The air forces, incredibly, were even more mismatched. The North Korean air force (NKAF) had 122 aircraft, primarily Yak-7s, for air-to-air combat and the famous Ilyshin IL-10 "Stormovik" ground-support aircraft, both designs being battle-tested veterans of World War II. The South Koreans had only twelve aircraft, all of them either trainers or light observation planes. Thus, for the opening days of the war, the stage was set not only for a rout on the ground, but for a series of punishing assaults from the air.

2

FIRST CONTACT

It started on Sunday, June 25, 1950, when 90,000 North Korean troops flooded across the 200-hundred-mile-wide border with the South. The North Korean troops, a well-trained cadre outfitted with Soviet weapons, artillery, and T-34 tanks, sliced into the ill-prepared and surprised Republic of Korea Army, tore it apart in the opening moves, charged straight into the capital of Seoul, and kept right on going.

Refugees from the invasion, American military wives, children (the attack had been so unanticipated that nonmilitary and noncombat personnel had not been evacuated), embassy families, and non-Korean civilians poured into Kimpo airport, in the suburbs of Seoul. The center of the city, little more than ten miles away, was already a battlefield.

United States Air Force transports had been coming in since the morning the war started in order to evacuate people back to Japan. On the second day of the war, two Yak-9s strafed the airport, flaming a fuel depot, destroying the control tower, and tearing up a C-54.

On the third morning, the American air force was

waiting. Flying top cover at 10,000 feet were five of the twin-body Mustangs, the F-82s, with four F-80 jets providing additional support five thousand feet higher up.

The Yaks, five of them this time, came in for another shot at the crowded airport and apparently did not even see what was ready to pounce from above. The F-82s dove in, nailing the Yaks before they even gained the outer edge of the airport, dropping three of them within a couple of minutes. The other two fled. Lieutenant William Hudson was credited with the first aerial victory of the war.

An hour later it was the turn of the F-80 Shooting Star. For the first time in the history of the United States armed forces, American combat jets went into action against an enemy air force. Eight IL-10 Stormoviks, the dreaded "flying tank" of World War II, approached the same target.

Four Shooting Stars broke out of their pattern above the airport and dove in for the kill. Captain Raymond Schillereff led the attack, tucking in behind a Stormovik. One quick burst and his target spiraled in and crashed, thus giving him credit for the first air-to-air kill by an American jet. Within seconds three more Stormoviks were down, two of them nailed by Lieutenant Robert Wayne. The survivors broke off their attack and fled north. Since American forces were only authorized to fight defensively, hot pursuit back to the base of the aggressors was not offered. The airlift out of Kimpo continued unmolested, with nearly 800 people flown out by the end of the day. In short order the field was abandoned, those still on the ground joining the columns of hundreds of thousands of refugees heading south.

America had entered the air war over Korea.

Within days two aircraft carriers, the American *Val-*

ley Forge and the British *Triumph,* were off the coast, adding their firepower to the struggle, and FEAF (Far East Air Forces) were authorized to fully engage the invaders.

Intimidated by their first encounter over Kimpo, the North Koreans were leery of committing their aircraft to offensive operations in the south. On July 3, over a hundred enemy aircraft were spotted at an airfield outside of Pyongyang, and, in a combined air force, navy, and British operation, navy Panther jets saw action for the first time. The series of raids all but destroyed the North Korean air force, leaving them with less than a dozen flyable aircraft. The Koreans would rebuild their air fleet, and soon be joined by the Chinese and the legendary Russian "Honchos," but for the moment this reversal granted breathing space to the allied forces, giving them undisputed air superiority over the entire theater of operations, a crucial advantage that helped to stem the tide of defeat.

Duane "Bud" Biteman was sent into the air war over South Korea within days of the start of the conflict. The opening weeks would prove a harrowing introduction to the reality of war, confronting him not only with the ultimate test of his strength and courage, but bringing him face-to-face with troubling moral questions as well.

Lieutenant Colonel Duane E. "Bud" Biteman
USAF, Ret. 18th Fighter-Bomber Wing

"They Called It 'Just a "POLICE ACTION" ' "
Taegu, Korea, July 1950

At the outbreak of hostilities in Korea, South Korea's president, Syngman Rhee, had begged our President Truman for a fleet of F-51 Mustangs, because he was convinced that a timely show of air power by the South Koreans would discourage the North Korean troops. In response, on July 1, 1950, President Truman authorized the transfer of just ten airplanes. However, since all of the fighter units in the Far East had already converted to F-80 jets many months before, the only F-51s that were not mothballed and in storage were a decrepit few used to tow targets for aerial gunnery practice.

As Mustangs, they were derelicts. All had been stripped of instruments; they were dirty and they were "tired," but they were the only 51s in the Far East available for immediate use. Ten pilots of the 35th Fighter Group ferried those ten "Bout One" Mustangs to Taegu and, it's significant to note, they were called upon on their way over to fly top cover for General MacArthur's C-54 "Bataan," en route to Suwon, where he was to confer with General Dean and look over the battle situation.

It was notable that they chose the old derelict F-51s over the newer, faster F-80 jets, because the old Mustangs had enough fuel to stay over the field the entire time MacArthur was on the ground, plus enough reserve to escort him all the way back to Pusan and still return for their original intended landing at Taegu!

Upon arriving at Taegu, the "Bout One" commander, Major Dean Hess, and his crew set about trying to teach the inexperienced South Korean pilots how to fly the hot, frisky Mustangs from the rough "cow pasture" runway at Taegu. It was a hopeless task, trying to upgrade from a 650-hp T-6 trainer to a tricky 1,450-hp fighter while flying combat missions against the enemy—an impossible situation.

Understandably the Koreans were reluctant to take the strange airplanes low enough to make an effective attack, and one was badly damaged by ground fire in just the first couple of days. The "Bout One" pilots couldn't bear to see the air capability wasted while they were so badly needed in the fighting, so they just left the Korean pilots on the ground at Taegu to refuel and re-arm the airplanes, and they started flying the combat missions themselves.

By the time our "Dallas bunch" started arriving a day or so later with no airplanes of our own, Headquarters FEAF had decided to give us the nine remaining flyable 51s, complete with South Korean insignia painted on the wings and fuselage. Dean Hess and several of his "Bout One" pilots stayed on for less than a week, while our troops straggled in aboard our supplies from Japan. Then, when we had enough pilots on board, most (but not all) went back to their units in Japan.

Eventually, when more F-51s became available, Dean Hess's people moved to Masan on the southern coast to start a pilot training school for the South Korean pilots. Dean Hess later wrote a book of his Korean experiences, which was made into the very popular and profitable movie *Battle Hymn,* starring Rock Hudson.

Captain Jerry Mau, my old friend and flight commander, was standing outside our C-47's door when I arrived at Taegu on July 14, and, with a wide sweep of his arms, smilingly said, "Welcome to Taegu, Queen City and Honey Bucket capital of the Orient." One whiff of the pungent air and I immediately knew the brand of fertilizer the Koreans preferred for their rice paddies.

My eyes followed the sweep of his arm across the barren pasture. All I could see were six widely dispersed F-51s with South Korean insignia markings, one adobe building and an awninglike affair over a low stack of packing boxes (which housed our "maintenance hangar"). That was it! All of it! Off in the distance to the north, atop a steep hill, I could see a few one-man "pup tents."

While the C-47 was being unloaded, Jerry showed me the nerve center of our squadron: the Operations Office—one small room of the adobe hut with a local area chart thumbtacked to one wall, two or three wooden ammo boxes, and a hand-crank field telephone. He told me that Moreland and Hauver were off on a combat mission with two of "our" nine Mustangs someplace near Suwon, or wherever our front lines happened to be at the moment. The only other room of the adobe shack was occupied by a detachment of a half-dozen "Mosquito" pilots: spotters who flew the three assigned T-6 trainers with South Korean observers in the rear seats to help locate targets and try to tell us which troops were friend and which were foe.

Taegu airfield, in mid-July 1950, was an airfield in name only, and in the loosest possible definition of the word. It was simply an open patch of pastureland, approximately 4,500 feet in length, located 4 miles north of Taegu City. One small adobe-type building sat alongside the rice paddies on the north side, just below a steep hundred-foot hill. The "runway" ran east and west, and was little more than a dusty road with numerous chuckholes and many soft, sandy spots.

For some reason, I'd always had the impression that air wars would somehow be more "organized" than the unpredictable battles of the mud-slogging infantry; that an airfield required a certain amount of preparation before it could be made operational; and right along with the effort to prepare the runways and the "work" areas, there was always someone there in the background arranging for a reasonably comfortable place for the aircrews to sleep and to eat.

After all, I had thought, if the pilots were to be in condition for the rigors of aerial combat, there would have to be facilities provided for them to get some rest between flights, some nourishing, if not necessarily "tasty" food, and maybe even an occasional cool brew.

Even in China in World War II, during our hop-scotching from one new fighter strip to the next, they always had us coming into bases with minimal niceties like a mess tent and eight-man sleeping tents with wood-plank floors. But then, as I thought about it, I realized that I'd never had the opportunity to get into a combat area right at the start of a brand-new war. And, as I looked around at the bleak, nonexistent facilities at Taegu, I wondered if I hadn't arrived in Korea too soon; maybe I could go out and come in again after they had things arranged more in the fashion that I had been led to expect!

Jerry showed the way as I balanced myself against the weight of my canvas B-4 bag. At the moment it contained all of my meager personal possessions—a couple of summer flying coveralls, two sets of starched khaki uniforms, a lightweight flight jacket, a half dozen sets of underwear, a couple of towels and washcloths, shaving kit and toilet articles, a writing kit, and pictures of my wife and daughter, Helen and Carol.

With my .45-caliber automatic pistol, holster, extra clips of ammunition, a first-aid kit and a canteen on the web belt around my waist, and a Leica camera slung over my shoulder, I was carrying everything I owned or would need in the line of personal supplies. We first went to a jumbled mound of olive-colored equipment, where I pulled out a pair of shelter halves and a couple of short rods for tent poles. As I started to walk away, Jerry suggested that I pick up one of the steel helmets from the pile "not so much for protection from gunfire," he said, but I'd need one for a washbasin and a bathtub.

Mau carried part of my gear as we picked our way carefully across two or three rice paddy dikes to the foot of the hill, which they'd nicknamed "Honey Bucket Heights," where the steep, eroded, and dusty path led to the top and "officer's country." There was a rutted road around the back of the hill, which would take us to the same place at the top, but it was a good half mile further around, and we soon got used to the shortcut across the narrow rice paddy dikes.

Scattered at the top was a random array of pup tents, straw mats, carbines, and steel helmets, looking for all the world like a combination beach party and "exploded" view of a Boy Scout camp area.

"Pick a spot," he said, "the rent is cheap, we have a nice panoramic view of the valley, and we're away from the strip, in case someone decides to strafe the runway." There was only one sign of "organized" civilization, a 12-foot-by-20-foot tent: the "Officers' Club and Mess Tent." As I expected, when I pulled aside the flap to peek in, it was just a big, empty tent with a dirt floor and a few B-4 bags strewn down one side. There was no "Club," and there was no "Mess Hall"; it was just a place to get in out of the sun to sit on the ground and open a can of army C rations.

It took me just a few minutes to find a reasonably flat spot and set up my pup tent. I pushed my bag inside, and we headed back down the trail toward the flight line. I was anxious to locate my Intelligence gear and find a corner where I could set up my chart rack and start collecting pilot reports; to see if I could plot a bomb line from the reports of returning pilots. I moved my Plexiglas-covered chart rack into the Operations Office and replaced the dirty, marked-up paper map that was tacked to the wall.

I asked a couple of the Mosquito pilots in the next room if they could tell me where the front lines were. They just laughed, and ran their fingers in a broad, sweeping arc across the entire middle of South Korea: "someplace between Suwon and Taejon on the west, between Hamhung and Wonsan on the east coast, and it's anybody's guess where it is between the two." The "front," if it could be called that, was moving south so fast that it was impossible to identify any specific area as being in friendly or enemy hands. Harry Moreland and Chuck Hauver returned from their combat mission and were a little more help. They'd been working over the roads leading into Taejon from the north, and that city had not yet fallen—not quite yet.

While I busied myself setting up my shop and locating my equipment from among the pile off-loaded from the C-47, a crew was busy setting up a field kitchen in a couple of tents under a few scrubby trees a hundred yards from our Operations shack, and a water trailer was brought in from Taegu. Civilization was coming, bit by tedious bit.

It was well after dark that night before I managed a dry sandwich from the field kitchen and trudged up the dark trail to Honey Bucket Heights and my little tent on the hard ground. Mine was an eerie feeling: lying on the ground, under the stars on that warm July night, I was dead tired but unable to sleep, wondering what the next few days, weeks, or even months would hold for us.

Weariness finally overcame my rambling thoughts, and I dropped off to sleep only to be shocked awake by the earsplitting chatter of automatic carbine fire nearby. Seconds later, another burst was heard from another nearby hill, then another from a third hill in the distance. I could see the flashes from the muzzle of the last burst, then silence as the darkness once again closed around us. At the first chatter of gunfire, I was wide awake and out of the tent, with my cocked .45 automatic in my hand, ready to do battle. "What a helluva way to start an air war," I thought, "a firefight against a bunch of trigger-happy guerrillas."

I could see nothing but our other pilots, all armed and ready to shoot at anything suspected of being an enemy. Slowly and carefully, we crept toward the spot at the far side of the hill where we'd last seen a South Korean army rifleman. When near enough to see his silhouette, standing relaxed near the top of the knoll, we recouped enough nerve to stand upright and walk over to find out what was going on. By sign language and pidgin Japanese, we found that there had been no enemy attack, the bursts of gunfire were just the guards' way of signaling each other that everything was okay!

There was little sleep for the pilots the rest of that night; just a lot of nervous jokes about how we joined the air force to stay away from just that sort of life.

Interrogation Tools—"Clues from the Brews"
Taegu, South Korea, July 1950

Typhoon Gloria swept across Japan on July 22, 1950, just a week after our arrival in Korea, and we'd caught the downpour of the fringes of the storm. We set up four 20-foot tents in the middle of our flight-line parking area. One was used for maintenance and supply storage, the second for our Operations Office, since we had promptly outgrown our limited space in the adobe shack and needed a place to store parachutes, life rafts, and other flying gear between flights.

The third tent became my Intelligence office, where I could brief the mission assignments and interrogate returning crews. The fourth tent became our "Pilot's Lounge," a place to lie down in the sultry shade to rest between missions. None were fancy—we had packing crates for chairs and tables, straw mats for cots—but it was an improvement over sitting under the wings of the fighters, trying to get a few minutes of relaxation. And it made my task of interrogation somewhat easier, because the returning pilots could be prevailed upon to sit for a few minutes, so that I could question and record the results of their missions and pass the information on to Fifth Air Force Headquarters. Their adrenaline was still flowing, understandably, when the pilots landed from an exciting, ofttimes scary combat mission; their nervous energy was not conducive to sitting and answering a lot of detailed questions.

Typically it was easy to get them to talk about the

mission. Each was anxious to tell it in "war story" fashion; to tell how rough it was and how close they came to getting their asses busted. But it was much more difficult to get them to recall an exact location of a certain event, or to estimate specifically how many trucks or tanks were seen at a certain target area, or to guess how many troops were seen in which location.

Even under the best of circumstances, with no one shooting machine guns at you from the surface, it's extremely difficult to see clearly while traveling at 350 to 400 mph and maneuvering 50 feet above the ground. It is more normal to concentrate on clobbering the enemy than counting them!

My friend, Lieutenant Don Bolt, formerly of the 67th Squadron at Clark, had been administratively "grounded" by the air force economy purges of the previous year and had been taken off of flying status, but he had been offered the chance to fly again if he would "volunteer" to fly combat in Korea. He jumped at the chance and sent word to me that he would be coming through Tokyo on his way to Taegu, in case there was anything I wanted him to pick up for me on the way over.

By that time I had found a need for a couple of storage lockers and asked him to pick up a couple of the nice aluminum footlockers available at the Tokyo PX. As an afterthought, I said that he might just as well fill them with as many cases of canned beer as he could fit into them. I would pay him for the whole works upon delivery.

When Bolt arrived with my two footlockers and *ten cases* of individual cans of beer—240 cans—I knew that I had found my answer to holding the returning pilots in the interrogation tent until I finished their mis-

sion critiques. I donated one free can of beer to each
returning pilot, as long as he would sit and answer my
questions while he consumed it. It was "weather
cooled" in the heat of July, but it was thirst-quenching
and refreshing, and above all, it was the *only* beer on
Taegu air base at that time!

World War II pilots in most theaters of operation received a one-ounce "shot" of "Mission Whiskey" upon
return from a combat flight. This, too, was one of the
neglected oversights of the early Korean air war. The
omission was not even considered by most crews, who
were much more concerned with the floorless tents,
cold showers from 55-gallon drums, and the shortage
of every conceivable item necessary to get a combat
F-51 into the air, including spare airplanes and pilots.
Reportedly the traditional liquid relaxant was eventually made available for the later Korean combat crews,
but the distribution did not commence until long after I
had completed my One Hundred Mission Combat Tour
behind enemy lines and left Korea eleven months later,
in mid-June 1951.

The ten cases of donated beer lasted almost two
weeks and, at the 1950 Tokyo PX price of $2.50 per
case, I figured it was $25 well spent to help me get my
postmission interrogation job done properly.

First Combat Mission, Flying the F-51
Taejon, South Korea, July 1950

The F-51 was fondly nicknamed the "Spam Can" because, from the side, the shape of its fuselage looked as
deep and flat-sided as the namesake tin can used for
packing the processed meat. In those days we, for a

fact, used the tin from Spam cans to patch bullet holes in the skin of our airborne Spam Cans (it's true, I swear!).

After my very thorough preflight check of the dusty, old World War II vintage Mustang, I climbed onto the left wing, pulled my backpack parachute on over my Mae West life-preserver jacket and over my pistol belt and holster, snapped the buckles, and cinched the straps to the point where they were "just uncomfortable" if I tried to straighten up. I then climbed awkwardly over the left cockpit ledge and sat on the one-man life raft, which had previously been placed in the seat "pan" by the crew chief.

Thick aluminum snap fasteners on each side of the life raft pressed into my thighs as I attached the "dinghy" pack to the metal rings sewn onto the side straps of my parachute harness. After reaching over and behind the seat back to pull the pair of shoulder straps across to my midsection, I carefully positioned the lap belt and snapped the lever to fasten all four ends of the shoulder and lap harness together.

With the added protrusion of the .45-caliber automatic pistol and holster on my right hip, I had to squirm my buttocks around until the holster hung outside of the seat bucket and, with the large, uncomfortable snaps of the dinghy harness pressing into each side of my posterior, I continued to squirm in the seat to get each cheek into its least uncomfortable position while I pulled the lap belt to a snug tension.

Finally, after plugging the radio cords into the wires from my hard-hat helmet, fastening the oxygen hose connection and clamping it to the shoulder harness, I placed my helmet astride the top of the windscreen.

With all of the necessary preliminaries completed, I could at last get about the business of starting the Mustang's big Rolls-Royce Merlin, 1,650-hp engine.

For all of its power and grace in the air, there are few wheeled contraptions more awkward than a tailwheel aircraft on the ground. It was as if the engineers, after designing a superbly efficient flying machine, conceded the fact that the ship must occasionally spend some time on the ground and very reluctantly agreed to hang on a set of three wheels. The main, front wheels, under the wings, had to raise the fuselage high enough to keep the big four-bladed propeller from striking the ground, and the small tailwheel had to be as compact and as light as possible in order to retract into the narrow aft section of the fuselage.

The resulting configuration meant that the pilot could not see over the nose while taxiing and had to continually turn the nose from side to side in order to see where he was going. Then, too, the placement of the main gear, close to the center of gravity in the wing, made it very risky to apply brakes too quickly, or the weight of the heavy engine would have a tendency to shift the balance forward with embarrassing and costly results, as the tail would swing up, and the propeller blades would dig a furrow in the turf or pavement of the taxiway. The invention of nose gears meant a major and dramatic improvement in the ease of the fighter pilot's chores.

Seoul's Han River Bridge
Seoul, South Korea, midsummer 1950

The impact of our repeated daylight fighter attacks became apparent rather suddenly during the last week in

July. Where the Reds had previously charged blindly ahead in full daylight—seemingly oblivious to the toll we were taking on their tanks, trucks, and troops—they suddenly began seeking concealment during the day, making their advances only at night.

As their forces neared the Naktong River, we really had to search hard for them, looking under each tree and inside the buildings of each village. They would drive their tanks right through the walls of several buildings in the village, then drive their trucks and tanks inside and camouflage the openings with net or straw so they would not be detected from the air. Or, if there were no villages nearby, they would park under a clump of trees and spread netting and branches over the equipment.

They made it necessary for us to drastically change our tactics, because we had to search out the targets at minimum altitude—literally lifting the branches of the trees to look underneath for their arms, or to find their tank tracks where they'd failed to cover them. There were just as many targets as there had been before, once we found them; but we started picking up more holes in our ships from small-arms fire while we were down on the deck searching for clues.

We therefore modified our tactics accordingly, by what came to be known as "yo-yo" maneuvers. Instead of two or more ships going in to search or attack a target simultaneously, we'd keep one ship high—above 2,000 feet—just high enough to stay out of much small-arms (rifle and machine gun) range, while the other went down onto the deck. Then, if the enemy fired on the attacking plane, the top cover could usually spot the muzzle blasts and be able to dive in to attack, while the first attacker would pull up to fly "shotgun," continuing the one-up, one-down coverage as long as there were targets in the area.

When we'd come across an especially lucrative or heavily defended target, one that we had to hit repeatedly, we'd try to vary the patterns to be sure that we never made our attacks twice from the same direction. To do so was to invite disaster, because the gunners were able to take a sighting on one ship, then be all set to blast the next one down the "chute."

Instead, we'd make sure that our attack headings were at least 60 to 90 degrees offset from the preceding ship and I, personally, would always let loose a short burst of machine gun fire just as I started in on the target, even at long, out-of-range distances—just to suggest the gunners put their heads down. They really didn't know whether I was shooting at them or not, so they'd often hold their fire for fear I'd see their muzzle blast and aim directly at them.

But as soon as we'd passed their position, and they knew we couldn't turn on them—WOW! All hell would break loose, and everyone on the ground would swing their guns around and try to get us on the way out, unless my wingman was coming down the slot at the same time that I was pulling off.

At any rate, I soon got into the habit of "jinxing" the ship around as I approached the target and especially as I pulled off. I'd push rudders, stick, and ailerons all over the cockpit, to keep the ship flying as *uncoordinated* as I could make it, and if there was a hill nearby, I'd roll over on my back and scoot over the hill close to the ground, rolling right side up only after I was on the opposite side, where the targets' gunners couldn't take aim at me.

Then, after a few miles or so on the other side, I'd

pull up steeply to trade my excess full-throttle airspeed for a couple thousand feet of quick altitude and start another attack from a far different angle. My defensive techniques worked very effectively for me, and, although most attacks were at low altitude in heavily defended areas, few gunners were able to successfully take a bead on me. My Mustangs picked up very few holes.

White Robes: Refugees or Reds?

By early August 1950, the momentum of North Korea's three-pronged drive into the south had proved immensely successful. They had completed their end-around on the west and south coasts, their east coast drive had progressed far enough to force evacuation of U.S. Air Force fighter squadrons from Pohang air base, and their central thrust was threatening to cross the Naktong River to knock out our last bastion of defense: our home base at Taegu.

Their objective, to surround Taegu, then march on Pusan and have control of the entire peninsula, seemed just a few days short of accomplishment. We were in deep trouble! Despite our intensive firepower from dawn to dark every day, we just didn't seem to have enough airplanes or pilots to properly stem the Red tide.

As our defensive perimeter continued to shrink around Taegu, we became suddenly aware of the mass exodus of Korean refugees ahead of the battles. But the full impact of their presence did not strike home to me until the first few days of August 1950, when the stream of white-clothed humanity began to collect on the west bank of the Naktong River.

Only then, as I sat in the narrow confines of my F-51's cockpit in relative "comfort," patrolling the river to prevent their crossing, did I begin to feel the weight of the decisions that were suddenly forced upon me—decisions for which my years of air force training had neglected to prepare me and that violently contradicted my Christian upbringing. Could I bring myself to fire my machine guns at those refugees in order to keep them from crossing the Naktong River?

We knew that the Red army troops had dressed many of their soldiers as refugees, who then infiltrated behind our lines to attack from the rear at opportune times. But we knew, too, that these thousands upon thousands of old people and young children had been forced from their homes in Seoul or Suwon, then from Taejon, Nonsan, and Kumsan, and all of the villages in between, carrying all that was left of their lifelong possessions. Many were Christians, for Korea had responded to missionary zeal for scores of years. I couldn't know how many could be praying to Jesus for deliverance at the exact instant that I was asking the very same Jesus for divine guidance; when the time came, I might have to pull the trigger on them!

The Naktong River near Hamchang was extremely shallow in August, shallow enough to wade in many places. We knew that these crossings must be closely watched, because these were the areas the North Koreans would attempt to cross. There was no question in our minds concerning our response to soldiers trying to cross the river. We would stop them at all costs. But the subject of refugees was something else. We had no orders, nor even firm "guidance" from higher headquarters on the subject; just a sort of a general unspoken consensus that our position at Taegu would be very seriously jeopardized if and when the mass of refugees crossed the Naktong River.

There was no doubt in any of our minds that the exodus would be heavily infiltrated by armed North Korean troops, against whom we could have little defense once they crossed the protective Naktong River. No one would take the responsibility to issue a specific instruction on just how the refugees were to be stopped.

What I saw on that one bright, early August morning mission caused me to pull up into a wide, sweeping left turn, to place my flight in a parallel line with the river, where I immediately dropped down until I was barely ten feet above the sand and a scant yard over the heads of hundreds upon hundreds of white-robed men, women, and children standing in the middle of the river. They stopped where they were, and ducked as we roared over, then those nearest the east bank scrambled forward, while most of the others stayed where they were while we circled low for another pass. This time, though, I fired a long burst of machine gun fire into the open water ahead of those who had stopped in midstream. They immediately jumped up and returned to the west bank; but as soon as I would pull up to a higher altitude for a wider, more comfortable circle, a few would start down the bank, intent upon crossing while they thought we were not looking.

Their bright white clothing stood out vividly against the reddish, sandy riverbed, and we could observe their movements quite easily. So I would quickly roll over into another low pass, firing into the water ahead of them as I went by, and they would turn back and run to the riverbank. I prayed that none would call my hand, and try to cross after seeing my warning bursts of gunfire, because at that point in time I honestly did not know if I could fire directly at them to stop their crossing.

We patrolled that shallow portion of the river for a couple of hours, circling the shallowest areas at 500- to 800-feet altitude, then dropping down to fire a short burst into the river whenever a few foolhardy souls started to move across. I knew that sooner or later some would defy my warnings, because the multitude on the bank continued to grow, and they didn't dare stop moving while the battle lines continued to draw nearer in the west. The mental anguish of those couple of hours, sitting alone in my cockpit as I played "God" to those thousands of homeless, defenseless dregs of humanity, was the heaviest burden I had ever been forced to bear—or ever would!

It had been one thing to discuss various wartime tactics, distasteful or not, in a hypothetical context while seated in the detached atmosphere of the Operations Office—such as all agreeing that the refugees "must be stopped" if we were to save our position at Taegu. But, believe me, it was quite another matter to be sitting in the cockpit of a heavily armed F-51 Mustang, looking through the gunsight and searching my conscience for moral justification to pull the trigger on them. I prayed, fervently, that none of the refugees would challenge my warnings or if they did, I hoped some would suddenly uncover a machine gun or rifle and start firing at me, for only then would I have my needed justification. I had often strafed enemy troops, and I'd blasted their tanks and trucks with my rockets, without giving a second thought to the moral arguments of war and the "killing of fellow man." They were the enemy; they were paid to try to kill me at the same time I was attacking them.

But the refugees in their white costumes—they were something else: unknowns. They appeared defenseless, but were they? How many had rifles and submachine guns hidden under their long, white gowns, ready to attack our troops from the rear? I couldn't know. I had to just bear the anguish of uncertainty as I made pass after low pass, firing an occasional warning burst to keep them on the west side of the river—and hoping.

Courage, Valor, Heroism

Undeniably, for me 1950 and 1951 were vintage years for courage, valor, and heroism. And, while I was associated with the 18th Fighter Group pilots of those old F-51 Mustangs, I can proudly state that I ate with heroes, I drank with heroes, and, to a certain extent, a part of me died with many of those heroes. As a result of my Korean air war experiences, I am firmly convinced that valor and courage are not inborn; they are not hereditary. Instead, they are the result of their then-current environment: When you are surrounded by heroes, it is damned difficult not to perform like one!

Major Louis J. Sebille, leading a flight of 67th Squadron Mustangs out of Ashiya on August 5, 1950, wound up with but three airplanes when his wingman was forced to return to Ashiya with a rough engine. Captain Martin Johnson, his element leader, with Lieutenant Charles Morehouse on his wing, split off as they approached the target area and were informed by the pilot of a T-6 Mosquito spotter, of a Red tank or armored personnel carrier holed up inside a couple of houses in the village of Hamchang.

The fact of enemy armor so close to our airstrip, on our side of the river, coupled with an equally strong, si-

multaneous drive from the north, near Yongchon, made
our military position at Taegu "very precarious," to say
the least. Lou Sebille was well aware of our situation,
and knew just how critical each of our fighter missions
would be that morning in early August . . . perhaps the
success or failure of our stand in Korea hung by the
thread of his fighter's contributions. The T-6 fired a tar-
get-marker smoke rocket, which lit near the huts holding the Red armor and, at that moment, their Red crews
knew that they would soon be under air attack.

Sebille positioned himself for a medium-angle dive-
bomb run, planning to drop both of his 500-pound GP
[general purpose] bombs on the first attack. Diving
from 5,000 feet, he held the Mustang steady as he approached 2,500 feet altitude above the ground, then,
when the target passed under his nose, he punched the
red bomb-release button on his control stick to drop
the two bombs, one from under each wing. He immediately started a sharp pull-up to the left, to stay away
from his bomb blast, and called to his flight that the enemy was firing machine guns while he was making his
bomb run. Their element, meanwhile, was making an
attack on the other hut, a short distance from Sebille's
target.

Only one of Sebille's bombs had released on his
first attack, and the heavy 500 pounds of extra, unbal-
anced weight under his left wing may have contributed to his near-miss on the target. But the enemy
armor was still there, and was still firing its machine
guns at Lou's other element as they made their nearby
attack. Sebille climbed for another dive-bombing run
with his remaining bomb, making his attack from
south to north . . . the same direction as he had on his
first pass; he probably intended to pull the manual

bomb-release handle, to be sure of getting the bomb off.

Lou had a clear view as he came down the slot for the second time, but he also gave the Red gunners a clear shot on him as he did so. During his second attack, from a lower angle than the first, puffs of smoke were observed coming from the tank's cannon as well as from the machine guns and, just before he reached the release point, Lou called over the radio that he was hit. But instead of releasing his bomb at that point, he pulled up sharply to the left once more and, with a garbled comment over the radio that ended with "I'll get those dirty bastards . . . ," he continued his turn and dove straight toward the armored carrier. This time he fired his six rockets in salvo, and his machine guns were blasting the whole way down, but instead of pulling up as he reached the 2,000-foot danger level, he continued to bore in to 1,000 feet, then 500 feet . . . he obviously had no intention of missing his own bomb blast, for he dove his airplane and his remaining 500-pound bomb straight into his target. There was a tremendous explosion. . . .

Lou Sebille had, to be sure, "got the bastards . . ."!

"Why?" we asked ourselves, over and over, when we heard the account of his dive into the target. Why didn't Lou pull off the target and head for our nearby strip at Taegu, less than five minutes to the east? Knowing Lou as we did, we concluded that he must have been hit by one of the cannon bursts, and was so badly wounded that he knew he would not be able to land the airplane and still survive. And, since he knew he was undoubtedly going to die, he was determined that those who caused his death should die with him. And they did. A year later I saw the heartrending pho-

tograph of Jane Sebille, Lou's pretty young widow,
and his young five-year-old son, "Flip," standing on
the apron at March Field, California, while Air Force
Chief of Staff General Hoyt S. Vandenberg presented
the Medal of Honor and the flag, earned by Lou on that
August morning at Hamchang, in far-off Korea. *Time*
magazine's editors wondered in print if the young Sebille boy would ever understand why his dad never
came home; I had to wonder, too. In fact, I wonder if it
is possible for anyone to understand Lou's feelings on
that sunny, dusty Friday morning along the Naktong
River . . . so far away from his home and family in
Chicago.

Luck's Thin Thread, August 1950

On August 29, 1950, while our ground troops were still
locked in the battles around the Pusan Perimeter, I was
assigned to fly another long five-and-one-half-hour
"ass buster" from Ashiya, Japan, to the area north of
Pyongyang, the heavily protected capital city of North
Korea. Despite the tedious, long hours in the cramped
little cockpit of the F-51 Mustang, it turned out to be
an exceptionally good mission; I was able to destroy
two locomotives, one howitzer on a flatcar, several
boxcars, four trucks, and about twenty enemy troops.
But the troops almost got to me in the process.

It happened near Chorwon as I flew south looking for
targets of opportunity. I'd found the four trucks heading out of Pyongyang and was able to destroy them all
with just my machine guns, saving my rockets for

something more lucrative. And a prize it was: a locomotive with a half dozen boxcars about to enter a short
mountain tunnel. There was little room to maneuver in
the narrow canyon, but as I dove to intercept I knew
that I could get a fairly straight shot into the tunnel
from the far side by flying down the railroad approach,
then pulling up at the last instant to just clear the hills
above—and that's just what I did.

I got a beautiful six-rocket launch right into the tunnel to destroy the locomotive, but as I pulled up I could
see a machine gunner on the ridge above, peppering
away at me the whole time I was coming down over
the track. I didn't feel any hits, however, and, since I
was almost out of ammunition and fuel, decided to
head back to Taegu rather than challenge the machine
gunner on the spot. The thirty-minute flight back to our
staging base was uneventful, and upon taxiing up to
the rearm-refuel parking area, the line crewman
chocked my wheels as I shut down. He then climbed
up to help me unstrap and climb stiffly out of the tight
little cockpit.

Our oldtime, reliable line chief met me and was already starting to remove the engine cowling on the left
side of the nose. I promptly told him not to bother; that
the airplane was in good shape—"running like a fine
Swiss watch." With a friendly, knowing smile, he mo-
tioned me to come down by the nose to take a look at
my "fine Swiss watch." When I'd stepped down from
the leading edge of the left wing onto the tire, I could
then see a very long, narrow-angle slit in the cowling
that, when projected by the angle of its penetration,
was found to be aimed just very slightly forward of the
cockpit.

With the cowling panel removed, we could see

where the slug—a steel armor-piercing .50-caliber bullet—had missed my coolant line by a scant fraction of an inch. It had gone through and shattered a large section of the heavy aluminum I-beam bracing, which supported the left side of the engine, then had struck the engine block and penetrated to a depth of almost a quarter of an inch before stopping to drop into the cowling below. We found two or three shattered pieces of the enemy's projectile still resting in the lower cowling. We never did find the third piece, the tip. We assumed it must have shattered into several smaller bits when it hit the engine block.

I had been very, very, *very* lucky. Had my speed been just a fraction faster as I pressed my attack against the locomotive, that single bullet would have come into the cockpit at an angle that would have hit my chest. Had its angle been a bit steeper, it would have probably had force enough to penetrate and destroy my engine. And, if it had been but a fraction of an inch lower, it would have gone through my coolant line, causing the engine to quit before I could reach friendly lines. Or it could have destroyed the engine-mount I beam—any of which would have put me down behind enemy lines in short order!

I have saved those two broken pieces of that .50-caliber armor-piercing bullet—had them mounted on a key chain. They serve as a constant reminder to me of just how thin and fragile is the thread of "luck," and just how close I came to using my entire allotment on that day near Chorwon.

3

NEW PILOTS AND OLD

The first weeks of the war were a defensive holding action, trying to stem the tide of the Communist advance in order to buy time for the mobilization of a counterstrike. As quickly as air assets could be formed up they were immediately shipped across the Pacific to beef up the defenses and later in the summer provide air support for MacArthur's brilliant offensive at Inchon.

One of the first lessons rammed home to the American military in the summer of 1950 was just how much we had let our military preparedness slip in the five years after the end of World War II. Nearly everyone involved in the Korean buildup could remember how just a few short years before a dozen carriers with a thousand-strike aircraft on board or a fleet of 500 bombers could be moved in a matter of days and brought into action. Now it was taking weeks to wangle a score of fighters or one additional carrier for the desperate fight building up around Pusan.

Into this new war America funneled two distinctly different types of pilots, "the old hands," or vets of the

"Big One," and the untested pilots of the postwar generation.

For any fighter jock born just months or only a year too late to be in the greatest air war in history, the experience was a frustrating one. America had literally trained hundreds of thousands of pilots for World War II, tens of thousands had seen combat flying Mustangs, Thunderbolts, Corsairs, Lightning Bolts, and Hellcats. Thousands had stayed on after the war, the best of them surviving the cutbacks and graduating to the F-80, the heavier F-84 Thunderjet fighter-bombers, and the new agile F-86 Sabres.

A pilot who earned his wings anytime after the spring of 1945 walked and flew in the shadow of giants. The newer pilots might be more technically versed and skilled, being younger they might have sharper reflexes, in some rare cases they might even have higher rank, but they were still, in the eyes of the veterans, untested.

One can well understand this attitude, for after all these were men who had flown through the flak-blackened skies of Berlin, hunting for fights with the aces of the legendary Luftwaffe, or had penetrated into the heart of the Japanese empire and gone head-to-head with the samurai pilots of the emperor. Anybody who had not been through that test, no matter how well they flew, no matter how much they knew about aerodynamics, simply had not passed the final test.

Those who had been there knew the inner truths of the experience; those who had not, didn't and would be reminded of it on almost a daily basis. Thus when war erupted on the Korean Peninsula, there was more than one pilot eager to go, if only to prove to their comrades that they were fit to join the ranks of the elite and be called a combat pilot.

Frederick "Boots" Blesse was one of them, going into action at the same time as the Inchon landings, and he got far more than he bargained for when he discovered on his first mission that the biggest hazard might very well be some of the guys on your own side.

General Frederick C. "Boots" Blesse (double ace, Korea and Vietnam)
18th Fighter Wing
Debut in Korea—Cartwheeling the P-51

I was at Nellis when the war started. I had missed World War II, because I was at West Point at that time. I had five years of training alongside guys who were in World War II. We were flying in F-80s and F-86s. It was so frustrating, because anytime you did something good—if you got on the guy or really maneuvered up there and "shot him down" or something—in the debriefing room, he'd just shrug his shoulders and say, "Yeah, that was okay, but that's not the way we do it in combat." He had been there, and you hadn't been there, so the discussion ended, and there wasn't anything you could say to him.

For five years I heard that, and I didn't ever want to hear it again. Then the war started. General MacArthur was talking about having us back by Thanksgiving— that this thing was going to be as short as heck. I thought, "Boy, I am not going to miss this one." I was flying F-86s then at Selfridge Air Force Base. I went in, and they'd gotten a requirement for one P-51 pilot.

I volunteered for it. Nobody would touch it with a ten-foot pole, but I wanted it.

So they sent me to Nellis, and I was supposed to go through P-51 RTU [reconnaissance technical unit] there. But when I arrived, there were no P-51s at Nellis! Apparently they were going to get some, but they hadn't gotten any yet—it was too early in the war. So they sent me through in the F-80. Now, I was already combat ready in the F-80 and also in the F-86. There were four of us in the same position. It was supposed to be a three-month course, and they graduated us in eight days. We did everything we were supposed to do, and they could tell that this was not a learning process.

We were at Nellis about eight or ten days, and off we went to the replacement depot at Fuju in Japan. We got there, and the guy said, "You're F-80 pilots." We said, "Yes, they sent us as replacement pilots." He said, "Jeeze, it's too bad you guys don't have any prop time, because we've got squadrons that don't have but eight or nine guys in the P-51 outfits. The jet outfits are overcrowded, because they're not sending us any propeller-driven graduates anymore—they're all jet people." I said, "Hey, wait a minute. I've got some P-51 time." I had about seven or eight hours, and I'd had about seven hundred hours in the P-47. The other guys had similar experience, so we said, "Okay, we'll take the props." We all went to the 18th Fighter Group—two of us to the 67th Squadron, while the others went elsewhere.

They flew us in a C-119, and they hadn't checked the weight and balance very well. We were in the back of the 119, and the pilot stalls it out about twelve feet above the ground on approach. It hit the ground with such force that it just bent the booms down to the runway. I mean, everything was flying around everywhere in the back—it's a wonder we didn't get killed.

We got off, and some guys met us from the outfit we were supposed to go to. They took us to lunch and said, "You're on the mission tomorrow morning, and you've got to get three hours and ten landings before you can fly combat."

They had me scheduled, and I went over to Operations. This guy introduced me to the P-51. It didn't have any tanks on it—it was a clean airplane. Now, I didn't have a lot of time in the 51—maybe five or six rides. Well, he showed me some things about the airplane, because this was a different model, and I wouldn't have remembered anyway. He said, "You go up and fly and, after you've been up a couple of hours, come back over the field. I'm going to take off and join with you, and we'll do a little bit of formation flying just to be sure you're okay there. Then you can shoot your ten landings, and that will be it."

So we did all of that. We finished, went back, and the guy briefed me on the next morning's mission. He said, "Now, we never fly the airplane at night. The gyro we have tumbles at 60 degrees, and we don't have any navigational equipment except for this thing they call a DeTrolla." That thing had a needle on it like a radio compass—and a radio compass is pretty good. It'll pick up a station, and the needle will swing around and point right to the station. But this was too early for that. They hadn't invented that yet. This was a De-Trolla. It would only go left or right. If the signal was on your left, the needle would go left, but you didn't know if it was left in front of you or left behind you. So they didn't fly at night, and they didn't fly in weather.

He said, "Now, tomorrow morning, the guy will come by about four o'clock and wake you up. You come down, get a briefing, and Intelligence will give you stuff. Then you get your weather briefing, pick up your Mae West and your parachute. By then, they'll probably call the whole thing off, and you'll go back to bed. You'll come back down around ten o'clock and fly." "Okay," I said, "that's fine."

And, sure enough, the guy was around about four o'clock. He woke us up, and it was drizzling enough to get you wet. We walked down to Ops and did all the things he'd said we were going to do. We waited for the call so that we could go on back to the quarters. Well, the call didn't come.

After we were about a half an hour overdue, the flight commander called up to Seventh Air Force and said, "What about our mission? Are you scrubbing us?" And the commander said, "No, not yet." Our commander then turned to us and said, "Well, we're going to go out to the airplanes. It's dark out there and it's wet, but it will be a good experience. We'll preflight the airplanes in the dark, so take your flashlights. When you get through, climb in the cockpit, put the cockpit down, turn the radio on, and check in with me on B channel."

So we got into the airplanes, wet and chilly. We tuned in the radio, and the leader was talking to Seventh Air Force. Finally I heard his voice octave go up about one notch. The guy says they're having a big firefight just north of Pyongyang, and they have to have some air-to-ground support up there by first light. Our mission was going to go. This was my first mission, and I thought, "God almighty, I'm going to go out here in the rain on a pierced planking runway at night and fly formation with this guy?" I'd never flown a P-51 in formation until that afternoon before. And, of course, all the flying I'd done in a P-51 was in a clean airplane, and this thing had napalm rockets and .50-caliber machine guns. It was loaded—you couldn't get a heck of a lot more on it.

After a lot of nonsense, we taxied out. I was the number two man, since I was on my first mission. I asked the leader before we took off, "Say, if we get separated, is there some kind of an instrument departure for this field?" He said, "No, there isn't any." Of course, everybody knew there was about a 2,000-foot range off to the south of us, and he said, "If you get separated, this is what you do. As soon as you get airborne, pull the gear up and count one thousand one and one thousand two until you get to eleven. At eleven, make a ninety-degree left turn, and you'll go through the saddleback."

There was about a 2,000-foot hill, and there was a saddleback where it dropped down for several hundred yards. You'd go through that saddleback. I thought that was pretty haphazard, but that's what you were supposed to do. We climbed up and went on the mission. We'd dropped the napalm and were getting ready to fire the rockets when we got a call: "Everybody return to base." Instead of going back to Pusan, we were supposed to go to a 3,700-foot cornfield just across the river south of Pyongyang. We were supposed to get rid of all our ammunition and munitions, go in there and land, and get fuel and more ammunition for another mission. At the end of the second mission, you'd fly back to Pusan.

So we headed for Pyongyang East, and the weather was really closing in. You could see straight down, but you couldn't see slantwise. We flew over the base, and the leader peeled off. Then I peeled off and number three and four. The leader starts letting down, and he says, "The visibility is only a hundred or two hundred feet. Everybody pull up and go around." We made about two or three passes, and we couldn't find the end of the runway.

There was a guy in what we called "Mobile Control." He arranged for some people to come out and put two 55-gallon drums with about a foot of oil in the bottom of them. Then they took a newspaper, lighted it, and threw it in on the oil, which burned. They took those two cans and set them about 100 yards apart on the very end of the approach end of the airfield. When we went around, we could see that. So we took our spacing again. The leader was landing, and I was landing on his right, back about a couple hundred feet. He touched down, and I touched down, and everything was fine. Then, out of the corner of my eye, I saw this six-by-six truck coming across the runway from left to right. The three guys in this truck were thinking that nobody in their right mind would be using the airfield, so they decided to drive from one side of it to the other. The first thing I thought was that Joe Lane, the flight leader, was going to hit that truck. All of a sudden, Joe goes out of sight, the truck is still there, and it became crystal clear to me who was going to hit the truck. I was too slow to go around, and I was too fast to ground loop it. I hit full right rudder, right brake, and I reached up and hit the battery and the mag switch, so that if something happened, it wouldn't burn.

About that time, the airplane really didn't change direction, it just changed the direction of the nose about

20 to 30 degrees when I hit the rudder and the brake. The airplane kept going straight, and the left wing hit the front end of the truck. When that happened, it threw the airplane around like a slingshot. The left wing hit the truck, and it swung it around with such force that the right wing got flying speed, bringing the airplane back up into the air—not really to fly, but just to get up there and fall back down.

Next thing I knew, I was about 30 or 40 feet off the ground. I can still remember that four-bladed prop going around and that airplane coming right straight down into the ground. It flipped over on its back and chugged along for 10 or 15 yards, then everything stopped.

I had a crash bar right behind the pilot's seat, and that crash bar was sticking in the ground. In fact, it was so far in the ground that it had pushed my head over on a 30- to 40-degree angle. I sat there for a minute, then I started moving my fingers and toes, and I thought, "Hell, I'm not even hurt. I gotta get out of here." The airplane was on top of me, and I was fastened in, unable to move—trapped between the ground and the top of the airplane.

So I sat there for a minute, thinking, and I felt something running down my back, toward my helmet. The first thing I thought was "Oh, man, I'm bleeding." Then it dawned on me that blood wasn't that cold. It was gasoline draining out of the fuselage tank, hitting me in the back just above the buttocks, then going down my back and into my helmet.

About the time that was going on, I heard voices outside saying, "Sit tight, chap, we'll get you out." I can remember yelling to him, "Don't worry about me; I'm not going anywhere!" Two airmen had apparently seen what had happened and ran out. One guy had a bayonet, and he sharpened the stick that the other guy had. The two of them got down on their hands and knees and dug a hole directly under the cockpit two or three feet across and three feet deep. And that was enough for me to fall out of the cockpit and into the hole, then shimmy out of there.

The only bad thing I got out of it was some burns from the hundred octane, since my helmet filled up, and the fuel went into my ear for three or four minutes. When I got out of there, I ran like a son of a gun, because I couldn't believe that airplane wasn't going to burn. I ran about a hundred yards, then turned around to look at the 51. It reminded me of somebody's cigarette in a calm room—how the smoke will go up in circles kind of toward the ceiling. That's what it looked like, except these were fuel fumes. Fortunately, they didn't ignite. We watched this for three or four minutes, and a jeep drove up. They took me in to Operations, and the guy said, "How do you feel? Did you get hurt?" I said, "No, I didn't." He said, "Do you want to fly?" I looked at him and said, "Yeah, that's what I came to Korea for!" He replied, "Okay, there's a flight briefing in the next tent. Go over there, because they need one guy."

I took off in a flight of four about forty minutes after the accident.

A Memorable Mission

In the P-51s I brought back an airplane that had about 140 holes in it. We had come across a battalion that was walking in the open in very bad weather. Our forward air controller had directed us over a mountain and, as we came down on the other side, sure enough, there was a road with enemy troops walking down. We fired rockets, then turned around and made another pass from a different direction, strafing lengthwise down the column. I guess we made five or six passes and almost completely destroyed the battalion. The army came in later and took over that area, and they said there were about 137 people dead as a result of the attack. They wanted to congratulate the two P-51 pilots who were there when it was too bad to fly.

Shortly after the Inchon landings, which flanked the Communist invaders in the South, forcing them to withdraw in headlong flight, Duane "Bud" Biteman (none the worse for wear after his near-death experience strafing a train inside a tunnel) was sent in to support the ground troops and had yet another "gray hair" encounter.

Duane "Bud" Biteman

Inchon Elation—Home by Christmas

On September 15, 1950, our army, navy, and marines conducted an audacious but highly successful seaborne invasion through the 18-foot tides at the port of Inchon . . . far, far behind the enemy's then current Pusan Perimeter front lines. We were cheered to hear that Kimpo airfield was recaptured on the first day of the offensive and that troops were moving to retake the city of Seoul. On the following morning, I was elated as I took off from our newly reactivated Pusan air base (K-9) with a flight of four Mustangs, into the low morning scud, which remained from the recent passage of Typhoon Kezia, searching for likely targets along the perimeter area west and north of our beleaguered former base at Taegu.

Our flight ranged northwesterly, following the Naktong River to Sonsan, just west of Taegu, where, as we topped the crest of the near bank, I absolutely could not believe what I found. A panic-stricken Red army was running headlong, trying to wade across the summer-shallow river out in the open, in broad daylight. And, for the time being at least, few slowed to shoot at us.

I maneuvered our four Mustangs northward a short distance to a flat, level area where we could swing around while remaining at low level, to position ourselves to release the eight napalm bombs onto the river upstream of the masses of North Korean troops, allowing the flaming, floating, jellied gasoline to spread and engulf the full width of the shallow river.

We separated into pairs for subsequent attacks, which we flew repeatedly back and forth along the riverbanks, strafing as we went, taking turns to keep from interfering with each other's gunnery patterns. The Naktong River was soon "flowing red," literally, with the blood of a thousand routed enemy troops.

Working my way still further north into a narrow canyon between two steep hills, I found a group of Red soldiers trying to pull a truck across the river on a small raft attached to a long cable stretched to the west shore. I was able to take a bead on the truck by simply turning a few degrees, then launched all six of my "big 5" rockets at one time. With but a short "whooooosh," the rockets hit the water several yards short of the raft, the exploding water tipping the truck into the water on its side rather than destroying it, while sending up a massive wall of muddy water to about a hundred feet in the air. The narrow canyon walls, rising sharply from the river, prevented my making any kind of evasive turn that would enable me to miss the sudden watery barrier that was directly in my path of flight.

I had never before flown into a watery barricade of any size, and had absolutely no idea what the impact force of my 325-mph speed would have upon the structure of my airplane—even had I been allowed more than just that short instant of time to think about it before running head-on into my self-induced hazard.

My instantaneous reaction to the problem was an immediate exclamation of "Oooooooh sheee-it! I've done it now!" while I pulled back on the control stick and ran head-on into the massive muddy-green wall of water.

With a great "splat," the windscreen was covered, and for a brief microsecond I was reminded of taking a car through an automatic car wash, then just as quickly I was through it and into the clear air on the other side, none the worse for the experience, except for a few more gray hairs than I'd had just a few moments before.

4

GOING NORTH AND
THE CHINESE COUNTERPUNCH

The landing at Inchon proved to be one of the most successful seaborne counterstrikes in the history of warfare. MacArthur's attack was a complete operational surprise and typical of the flamboyant general's ability to surmise the weak spot of an opponent and exploit it. The North Koreans had not even bothered to consider fortifying Inchon, believing that the treacherous coastline and deadly 18-foot tides would prevent any military force from daring to venture ashore.

Within hours after the start of the landing, allied troops were advancing unopposed into Seoul and retaking the Kimpo airfield while carrier-based aircraft provided close support and protection for the fleet. In a matter of days, this airfield was reactivated as a main base for support of the allied dash eastward to cut off the North Korean troops who were racing to escape the trap.

American air support tore into the retreating Communist forces. On September 27, 1950, MacArthur received authorization to launch ground military operations into North Korea, an order that would be bitterly disputed later, since it changed the entire complexion of the war and led United Nations forces into a bitter three-year campaign.

At the time, though, MacArthur's quest to take the war into the North was an entirely logical one. North Korea had engaged in an act of blatant aggression, making a raw power bid to destroy the government in the South. Their campaign had been fought with a display of cruelty considered extreme even for Asia. As the enemy was forced to retreat out of South Korea, clear evidence surfaced that tens of thousands of civilians had been tortured, raped, and murdered. Most of the southern half of the peninsula had been devastated. There was indisputable evidence as well that the North Koreans had systematically murdered South Korean and American troops who had fallen into their hands. If the 38th parallel was allowed to provide a safe haven for the beaten foe, it could be fairly assumed that once they had regrouped, the enemy would undoubtedly continue the conflict, since all offers to seek terms had been rejected.

Beyond those direct military concerns, one must also remember the mindset of the times. The men leading the war effort were all veterans of World War II, and many had served in World War I as well. The first war had closed out with a negotiated settlement, thus producing the fertile ground for the second and far more deadly conflict. World War II had been a total war, prosecuted until full and final victory had been achieved (though MacArthur adroitly stepped around the issue of total surrender by allowing the Japanese emperor to stay on the throne).

War for men like MacArthur had to be fought to an absolute victory. North Korea had clearly been the aggressor, the campaign had never been defined as simply a defensive action to preserve South Korea, and until North Korea submitted to the will of the United Nations the war must continue, if need be all the way to the Yalu River. In short, North Korea started it, and we were going to finish it.

As to the geopolitical considerations related to the newly created People's Republic of China, that had been a hot-button issue in the 1948 presidential and congressional elections. At the end of World War II, it had been assumed that our supposed ally, the Nationalist forces under Chiang Kai-shek, would eventually triumph over the Red army and Mao. Prior to the full explosion of World War II, Mao was driven out of eastern China, forced to engage in a grueling 6,000-mile retreat to the far western mountains. The war against Japan, however, had given him breathing space, and as the war with Japan shut down, the war between Chiang and Mao reignited.

By 1945, the American government realized that Chiang was as much a hindrance as a help to the efforts to keep China non-Communist. During the war he had revealed his venal side, pilfering hundreds of millions of dollars of aid, his corruption filtering down through every level of the government and military. Tens of thousands of American troops who served in China, primarily with the army and air force, returned home with stories of the unbelievable corruption of the Nationalist officers and government administrators. If effectively marshaled, China could have sent hundreds of divisions of troops into action against Japan; at best they put half a dozen divisions of high-quality troops in the field.

The American government, knowing of the problem, was forced nevertheless to continue support and also to try to cover for the thievery of their protégé. The total collapse of Chiang in 1948, though predictable to those on the "inside," was nevertheless startling. Retreating to the island of Formosa, Chiang would continue to shout defiance at Mao, promising that a counterattack and liberation were imminent. Given the immediate and full support offered by Stalin to this newest addition to the Communist bloc, along with the emergence of the Soviet Union as a nuclear power in 1949, none but the most rabid of anti-Communists believed that such an invasion was possible.

The question of "who lost China?" echoed throughout the 1948 election and still haunted America in 1950. China was our ally in the Pacific; it was the issue of China that started our confrontation with Japan and now, only five years after that complete and total victory, China was in the hands of the Communists. This debacle explains as well the sudden Communist conspiracy fever that swept our country, with dark wonderings of who had helped to betray China into the camp of the Reds.

Thus, though in hindsight the decision to push north might be seen as unnecessarily risky, at the time it would have been political suicide not to strike into the heart of North Korea in order to finish the job. Anything less would have been seen as weakness or, even worse, conspiratorial, with the intent of letting the Communists off so that they could re-arm for yet further acts of aggression. The prospect that China might intervene seemed remote. Mao was still struggling to consolidate power and would not want to risk the opportunity for an excuse by the United States to back a counterstrike by Chiang and the Nationalists.

Those with a deeper knowledge of the region also argued that there was actually a three-way paradigm at play in the region. China and Korea had been, for

centuries, political and even racial enemies and neither side would seriously consider supporting the
other. Russia, in turn, though an ideological ally to
both, would not tolerate a potential expansion by China
into the region. The one point conveniently overlooked
by all was the simple fact that in spite of their differences neither Russia nor China would tolerate an
American military presence on the Yalu or accept the
loss of face of a client state going down to total defeat.

Thus, when MacArthur received authorization to
press north on September 27, the fuse was set for an
explosion.

Air operations were unleashed with a vengeance.
Here was an opportunity for the United States Air
Force to prove once and for all that its doctrine of
strategic bombing was valid. MacArthur even authorized the use of a fleet of 100 B-29s to level Pyongyang,
but this operation was canceled over concerns about
civilian casualties.

Air force, navy, and marine aircraft paved the way
for the rapid allied advance into Korea, tearing into
retreating columns of troops, smashing up points of
resistance, and sowing panic in the ranks of the North
Korean army. The Korean air force had ceased to exist, so air operations were completely unopposed except for ground fire.

The problem encountered by the U.S. Air Force, in
terms of its hopes for yet again demonstrating the effectiveness of a strategic air-war campaign using left-
over B-29s from World War II, was that quite simply the
allied rush northward leaped forward far too fast.
Dozens of targets placed on the priority list for destruction were simply overrun before the B-29s could go in.

This is not to say that the aging B-29 was not a po-

tent weapon. Dozens of targets were annihilated all
the way up to the Yalu. By the end of strategic operations in late October, viable targets for the Super-
fortresses had ceased to exist. One crew returned from
a mission claiming that their intended target was already destroyed and they had simply loitered about
the area until finally a lone enemy soldier was spotted
riding a motorcycle. They chased him about, dropping
individual bombs, until one finally nailed the pathetic
target. On that day he was truly one of the unluckiest
men in North Korea.

On October 22, 1950, operations for the 22nd and
92nd Bombardment Groups were terminated, and the
B-29s were dispatched back to the States. The air war
seemed all but over.

The ground assault had already swept past the
North Korean capital of Pyongyang. A division of Republic of Korea troops was on the Yalu, and the rest of
the allied advance was anywhere from within sight of
the northern border of Korea to roughly a hundred
miles back from the river.

On the ground, though, and in the area of tactical
air support, there were dangerous indicators that all
was not as it seemed. Reports started to filter in that
troops other than North Koreans were appearing
along the front. Early in the morning of October 14
and again in the evening, two enemy aircraft swept in
on Kimpo airfield, strafed, and dropped several
bombs. Four Mustangs were dispatched to try to hunt
down these attackers, since it came as a surprise that
the North Koreans still had anything left in the air, let
alone an airfield inside Korea to operate out of.

Sweeping up as far as the Yalu the following day, the
four Mustangs faced a storm of antiaircraft fire from
the north side of the river, and one of the Mustangs

was brought down. Though MacArthur protested this intervention by China, from that day onward antiaircraft studding the northern riverbank tore into any allied aircraft approaching the river.

A far more dangerous indicator came on October 18, when over seventy-five Chinese Communist planes were spotted parked at an airfield north of the river but were gone the following morning. Incidents continued, climaxing on November 1, when six sweptwing jets crossed into Korean territory and engaged a flight of Mustangs. The Mustangs managed to evade and returned to their base reporting that MiG 15s were now in the fight.

On the ground the indicators were growing as well. The division of Republic of Korea troops that reached the Yalu River on the sixth immediately began reporting probing attacks and patrols from across the river. On October 26, an American army patrol snagged its first Chinese prisoner. Over the next four days nine more Chinese were dragged in.

On October 28, 1950, the storm hit, with a major Chinese assault force crossing the river and slamming into ROK positions along the Yalu, triggering a retreat back into American reserve positions.

All the warning signs were there, but still the highest command dismissed the reports, saying that they posed no viable threat to the overall UN operations. It is a fascinating moment, one which reveals yet again the strange duality of MacArthur, who could display a remarkable genius, especially when it came to offensive operations, yet at the same time maintain a blind spot leaving him open for disaster. This blind spot became evident when an enemy's actions did not fit into his paradigm or understanding. At such moments the threat simply did not exist, an example being his abysmal failure to react swiftly in the hours after Pearl Harbor, when he still had time to disperse his air assets prior to the opening Japanese attacks on the Philippines.

By the first week in November, allied forces were falling back under the increasing tempo of Red Chinese attacks. What had started out as squad- and platoon-level actions quickly escalated to divisions, corps, and full armies committed to combat from China. Allied protests were ignored by the Chinese, who held to the remarkable position that the men involved in this action were simply volunteers who had swarmed over the border by the hundreds of thousands in order to help their beleaguered socialist brothers to the south.

These hundreds of thousands, well supplied and well prepared for a winter campaign, slammed into American, Korean, and allied forces with a fury never before experienced by western forces. Suicidal ranks of thousands of Chinese troops would charge in, heedless of loss, overwhelming defensive perimeters.

Reports came in revealing that when overrun positions were briefly retaken, evidence was found of the mass murder of wounded and disarmed prisoners that made the incident at Malmédy during World War II's Battle of the Bulge pale in comparison. One marine unit reported finding the remains of wounded comrades who had deliberately been burned alive inside the captured trucks and ambulances they had been trapped in.

This campaign reveals yet again how Korea is now the "Forgotten War." Nearly as many men as were caught in the initial retreat of the Bulge were pulling out in this operation as well. The German advance during the winter of 1944 rarely got more than 50 miles into our lines; the Chinese onslaught would push us back over 300 miles. Only a handful of units were actually cut off at the Bulge, and in the case of the 101st Airborne's defense of

Bastogne, those troops were deliberately sent forward with orders to dig in and hang on. In Korea entire divisions of allied troops were completely cut off and had to carve a path back out, and for the only time in modern American military history, troops had to be evacuated by sea pursued by hostile forces. Casualties exceeded the losses sustained during the pullback from the Bulge and our troops, often ill equipped, had to march out, bringing their wounded with them, through howling blizzards with temperatures dropping to forty below zero.

It was the American equivalent of the French or German retreat from Moscow. In terms of morale it was even more staggering. Only weeks before, troops had been promised that they were in the closing stages of a mop-up operation and that they would be on their way home before Christmas. Beyond that, this was not a war to save America from fascism, or to punish an aggressor for the sneak attack at Pearl Harbor, it was supposed to be a "police action."

Six months earlier few of the men had even heard of Korea and many of them, veterans of World War II, were simply in the reserves as a way of adding a few extra dollars a month to their income. Being mobilized to freeze to death in Korea was simply beyond their comprehension a few months before. Police action or not, it was still a war that had suddenly turned extremely deadly and except for the silver birds flying overhead, it seemed as if death was closing in as the Chinese hordes pressed the attack.

As our armies reeled back in retreat (though one marine commander gained fame for declaring that we were simply advancing in the other direction), it was our air units, flying round-the-clock support, which pretty well saved the day and with it the lives of tens of thousands of American and allied troops caught in the debacle.

Colonel Bill Myers with the 18th Fighter Group was caught in the middle of this chaos and retreat, laying his life on the line to save his comrades slugging it out below, and experienced firsthand the confusion created by the Chinese onslaught.

Colonel Bill Myers
18th Fighter Wing, 67th Fighter Squadron

I loved flying the 51. I didn't care much about flying combat over there, because I flew P-47s in World War II—Thunderbolts—and every time I took off I'd say, "Please, God, make this a Thunderbolt." But the 51 did me real good. To show you how good the 51 was—not better, but I mean good—I saw a big haystack in a little bitty field, and I thought, "God, that's a big haystack in that little field." So I gave it a little squirt, and it was actually a camouflaged ammo truck. It blew up, I went straight through it, and the airplane brought me home.

First Encounter Between Mustangs and Chinese

We were at Kunu-ri Gap. I flew the last and the first missions. The Chinese came down [from across the Yalu], and this army was coming down the road down that valley to the Kunu-ri Gap. It was getting dark, and the convoy was just jammed up—being shelled from each side. A guy named MacArthur [not to be confused with *the* MacArthur] was a controller right there at Kunu-ri Gap where the road went around—two ridges came down and the road made an "M" around them. MacArthur called us in and said that he was on a jeep right against the bank. He said, "Drop your napalm explosive as deep as you can." So I went in and dropped my napalm, but I didn't want to hit the jeep.

As I pulled up, he said, "That's too far away." Number two was coming in, and I thought his napalm was going to hit the jeep that was just above the bank. I flew up there to drop another load, and MacArthur said, "Yup, that's just right. I can feel the heat."

We dumped all our load up that ridge beyond where his jeep sat. The next morning I was on the first mission. We went up, and there was nothing but burned-out American trucks [abandoned and destroyed due to the speed of the Chinese offensive] right there where the Gap was, clear on up to the next river. It was about 30 miles of trucks. Very few of the guys got out, and those went over toward the ridge along the coast. But they wiped out the whole Chinese division.

MacArthur walked out . . . he was the only one. His driver didn't get out. He just went back over the ridge someway. You know, after our strike I guess a hole opened up and he got away.

Then the next evening we were at Chongjin, and our army . . . limbered up and were pulling out and we asked if they were going up to the top to stop the Chinese, and they said, "No, we're leaving." So our army left, and that night the Chinese were down at the river and we put all our crew chiefs in perimeter defense.

The next morning we evacuated. We loaded two trains with our stuff, then the train crews sabotaged one that didn't get out. So we had one train of our stuff left. We got all the airplanes ready to fly out, and about that time we got some F-82 twin-boom fighters to come in and fly our enlisted men out. After we took off, we went back and strafed the base and could see the Chinese sitting up on the hill waiting for us to leave so they could come in. It was quite a debacle.

5

BUGGING OUT

It *was* a debacle. Yet, in the midst of defeat, the retreat out of North Korea stands as well as an unsurpassed record of heroism on the part of the United States Army and Marines who, in the depths of a Siberian winter, pulled out from the Yalu and embarked on a fighting withdrawal back below the 38th parallel. Most of the units fell back down through the central mountains of North Korea while those on the eastern flank, cut off by the rapidly advancing Chinese, fell back on to the eastern coast, where they were withdrawn by sea, this operation being covered by carrier planes and aircraft staging out of Japan and United States Marine air units.

In addition, thousands of tons of supplies had to be dropped to cut-off units who were valiantly struggling to regain allied lines as the Chinese tidal wave swept around them. In a move never before tried in the history of any air force, an entire prefabricated bridge, each section weighing two tons, was dropped from C-119s down to the 1st Marine Division so that they could span a 1,500-foot-deep gorge, thus opening the way for their retreat back to the coast and eventual evacuation by sea.

Under nearly impossible conditions, transports landed on makeshift fields and straight sections of roads across North Korea, airlifting out thousands of sick, injured, and wounded who otherwise would have been left behind to the barbaric treatment of the Chinese.

On December 5, 1950, the North Korean capital of Pyongyang was abandoned. Tens of thousands of civilians, sick to death of the repression of their previous masters, left to join the shivering throngs heading south with the retreating armies. As the city was taken, thousands of civilians who stayed behind and were suspected of supporting the United Nations effort were brutally massacred.

The Chinese, smelling victory, forged ahead regardless of the punishment inflicted from the air. Vast columns of Chinese troops were caught in broad daylight, openly marching on main highways, and continued to advance even while being strafed and bombed. At night columns of trucks, headlights blazing, pushed down from the Yalu in a desperate effort to keep the hordes of infantry supplied with ammunition. The Chinese had gone into action well supplied with ammunition and food but were expected to forage for the latter once it ran out.

Though foolhardy, this pressing on regardless of loss helped to maintain pressure on the retreating allies and demonstrated as well the fanatical resilience of the Chinese infantry. Reports from prisoners indicated that upwards of half of the Chinese troops were suffering from severe frostbite a month into the offensive, but nevertheless were expected to stay with the army and continue to advance. More than one pilot, when observing this unstopping human flood from the air, likened it to army ants on the march or a scene from a Hollywood biblical epic.

General Stratemeyer estimated that the punishing air attacks raining down on the Chinese inflicted over 30,000 casualties during the first thirty days of the offensive from the North. Though the massive air strikes hindered the overall assault, they did not stop it. This is not to say that air power was ineffective, particularly when called in at nearly point-blank range, in turning back the Chinese swarm attacks threatening to overrun the cutoff and hard-pressed units.

Repeatedly it was the sudden appearance of B-26s, F-82s, Corsairs, Skyraiders, and Mustangs, swooping in like the cavalry of old, which turned back suicidal attacks that threatened the beleaguered American and allied troops. Lifesaving rings of napalm guarded the flanks and rear of retreating columns and cleared the road ahead. Without the air superiority maintained throughout the retreat, the withdrawal out of North Korea would have turned into the worst disaster in American military history.

Making the operational nightmare even worse was the fact that all the airfields captured in the North, or constructed in the wake of the autumn advance, had to be abandoned. In some cases, notice to evacuate was given with only a couple of hours lead time. Tens of millions of dollars of support equipment, laboriously moved north, were set afire or blown up. In other cases, ground crews were loaded into the second cockpit of F-82s or jammed into the bomb bays of B-26s, the Chinese closing in even as the last plane lifted off.

In the mass confusion of the retreat, a fair portion of the equipment successfully loaded onto trucks was lost anyhow. The roads leading south from Pyongyang to Seoul were jammed bumper to bumper with traffic (yet another reason why the maintaining of air superiority was essential). If a truck broke down or ran out of fuel, it was pushed off the side of the road, its cargo set afire, and abandoned. Wounded, frostbitten, and exhausted troops naturally received the highest priority, and millions of dollars' worth of equipment was ofttimes dumped to make room for the far more precious human cargo.

Of that retreat one historian later commented that not since the anguish of Valley Forge have American troops suffered such appalling winter conditions. The 38th parallel was not a stopping line for the Red counteroffensive. By Christmas allied troops were essentially back to the line where the war started in June. But the retreat was not yet over as the enemy continued to press the advance. Seoul fell yet again, this time suffering even more damage and the murder of thousands of innocent civilians.

As the allied forces fell back into South Korea, the Chinese continued to press the assault despite the air attacks. The Chinese launched a major attack on January 1 into South Korea, but the weather cleared and the Fifth Air Force and carrier-based aircraft launched round-the-clock sorties.

Using heavy Mark VIII flares, originally designed to illuminate wide stretches of ocean for air-sea rescue and antishipping actions, the air force deployed "Lightning Bug" C-47s. Dropped by parachute and lighting off at 5,000 feet, the Mark VIII illuminated several square miles of ground with a near-daylight intensity. Then B-26 night intruder units tore into advancing columns. Prisoners later admitted that this new tactic slowed the traditional night advances of the Red troops to a crawl. The C-47 illumination units would become a standard feature along the front for the rest of the war.

Beyond the round-the-clock poundings administered from the air, resupply for the retreating armies had to be maintained as well. The rapid retreat had resulted in the loss of thousands of trucks that would take months to replace. The roads leading across the border and into South Korea had been torn apart by earlier actions, and it was now the dead of winter. In short, the transportation infrastructure was a shambles, and the only way to maintain troops in the field was through resupply from the air. Cargo Command brought in over 12,000 tons of supplies and replacement personnel and evacuated over 10,000 casualties, while an additional 2,000 tons were dropped by parachute from C-119s.

After-action reports and interrogation of prisoners indicate that Red losses from air attacks approached 20,000 during the January offensive. It is conservatively estimated that from the start of the Chinese attacks in November till the burning out of the offensive at the end of January, well over 60,000 Chinese and North Korean troops fell to allied air attacks.

War is always a process of combined arms and services, and no one should ever dismiss the valiant efforts of one branch in order to praise another. It is safe to say, however, that without the unstinting efforts of airmen flying over Korea during the winter of 1950–1951 the retreat out of the North could have been the worst disaster in American military history. Airpower made the difference and helped to save the day.

The buildup of allied supplies, personnel, and logistical support finally stopped the Chinese onslaught. By the end of January, the Chinese high command conceded that the offensive was spent and could not hope to be resumed until spring due to extremely heavy losses, destruction of equipment, the near-total destruction of the transportation infrastructure in North Korea, air interdiction, and the outrunning of their own supply net.

The combined air forces of North Korea and Red China had played little if any role in the offensive except for occasional harassment raids. Red air assets were rarely encountered at this stage of the war south of Pyongyang, though the airspace above the Yalu River was heavily defended by MiGs basing out of China. Throughout the operation there is no clear evidence of Chinese aircraft providing direct tactical support at the front once United Nations troops fell back below Pyongyang.

With the dying out of the Chinese offensive in January, United Nations forces pushed back, doggedly engaging the Chinese over ground that had already been fought over three times before. Seoul was in complete ruins by the time Chinese and North Korean forces were driven out yet again. In this bitter combat of slowly retaking South Korean territory, air units provided close-in tactical support and ran interdiction missions to cut enemy supplies.

Colonel Ralph "Salty" Saltsman was there with the 18th Fighter-Bomber Wing, providing top cover for the troops and engaging the enemy on the ground during this bitter late-winter and early-spring counteroffensive.

Colonel Ralph "Salty" Saltsman
18th Fighter-Bomber Wing

Early Days of the War and Getting Jumped by MiGs

I got to Korea in early spring of '51 and left in November of '51. We were flying F-80s in the Philippines, but they took those and gave the first bunch who went to Korea P-51s to fly escort. They had a bunch of them in storage, so that's how we got into the P-51 business early. There weren't very many MiGs flying when I first got over to Korea. They didn't come on strong until later. We just didn't get much air-to-air with them.

We had control of the air even after the MiGs arrived, thanks to our F-86s. Before the MiGs arrived, the North Korean Air Force was all we had to contend with. They did use the MiGs in a supporting role, however, and occasionally you'd run into a few even early on. The North Koreans had a business of flying biplanes at night. They'd come around and harass our advance bases, because they could fly by the seat of their pants. They dropped mortars and hand grenades and just raised dickens. But in the air, the MiGs were the serious contenders. We did get bounced by them a couple of times.

We were out on a rail-cutting mission one day with three or four flights of P-51s. We'd generally go on rail cutting and try to interdict their transportation system by dive-bombing with 500-pound bombs to cut the rail. We had to go to work at night. In the course of setting up for this mission, one MiG—at least one—busted through our formation. Before we had time to appraise whether we were going to get bounced by more, I told my flight to clear out their ordnance and get rid of their bomb load. In this case, we had six rockets. When the flight out in front released his, he released them toward the MiG. The rockets had proximity fuses on them, and those were meant to burst ten or fifteen feet from the target. Well, this thing went off, and I guess it scared the MiG so much that he just turned tail and went on back over the Yalu. He figured the 51s were shooting some heavy artillery at them!

That was just one incident. They were very rare, really. They'd follow us in on dive-bombing missions and try to pick off the last guy if they could get him. The MiGs couldn't turn inside us, so we had confidence that if we had to turn around, we'd get a shot at them. But we never lost significantly to the MiGs. They left us alone, because they didn't want to get around low altitude, where we were doing most of our work.

P-51 Against a Russian Fighter-Bomber

Another time, I got involved in a special mission that I'd heard about down at my main base, K-10, at Chin Hae. That night, I flew on up to K-16 for the mission. They sent out a squadron, and I had a flight. In this particular case, it was reported that some aircraft were going to attack one of our islands off the west coast, south of Sinuiju and north of the Inchon area. We were fortunate. We got the altitude on them as we went in, and I found out that they were Stormoviks, the Russian fighter-bombers that were very well armored—though I didn't know about the armor until later. They had used them with great success against the Luftwaffe on the eastern front during World War II. There was a pilot with an observer-gunner in the backseat.

I got into a good tail position below the gunner, and I put considerable ammo—800 rounds, in fact—into the plane, not realizing he had armorplate up there. Finally I got his oil, but I didn't see any flames—just a windshield full of oil. I had to break off, since I had no visibility whatsoever. The 51 was just coated with oil. My wingman had broken as soon as I made the attack, so I had to get the heck out, and I never did find out the fate of the enemy plane. I had to submit a probable and couldn't claim a kill. Our Intelligence people said it was an IL-2, but I have no idea. We also never knew if the pilot was Russian or Chinese, but we certainly had intelligence that there were some Russians flying for the Koreans.

P-51 Missions

One day—April or May of 1951, north of Seoul—it was reported that the Chinese were crossing back over the Inchon River. It was a game—they'd advance, and then they'd get driven back. In this case, they were coming over and had underwater bridges—bridges strung about three feet under the water—and they'd cross over on those things. Once on the bank, they'd mass again. It was just like one of those shooting galleries. You'd get down and see all these guys with their camouflage on, and you'd gun them off the bridge. Our napalm and rockets would get the mass of troops on the other bank. They later gave us a count from the controller, and it was about 1,800 or 1,900 troops we'd killed, which wasn't bad for a flight of four. Every day, you had to stand alert for the ground controller and just go after whatever targets he had. We went after all kinds of things—vehicles that they'd cover over with haystacks and such, road cuts, rail lines—it was all kind of a cat-and-mouse game to keep the Koreans from moving troops and supplies up.

6

PUSHING BACK

Air operations throughout the spring continued at an unrelenting pace, shutting down only when weather made flying impossible. Colonel "Pancho" Pasqualicchio, flying with the 18th, faced the experience most dreaded by any pilot, getting shot down behind enemy lines. Fortunately, there was a new tool in the arsenal of the United States Air Force, the helicopter.

Helicopters had actually been deployed into combat during World War II. The Germans introduced their first combat model in 1944, and by the last months of the war it was being used extensively as a courier, transport for high command, reconnaissance, medical evacuation, and the rescue of downed pilots behind the Russian lines.

America had deployed several hundred choppers as well by 1945, for use primarily in Burma and the Philippines, where they were found to be ideally suited for evacuation and rescue work. The early machines were barely capable of lifting a pilot and a single passenger, but were ideally suited for work in the jungles and mountainous terrain of the CBI [China Burma India] and the Philippines, where it was all but impossible to cut out a landing strip solely for the rescue of a single pilot or the evacuation of a couple of wounded.

By 1950, choppers had been improved somewhat in terms of lift capacity, and by the end of the Korean conflict the first experiments were being made in its use as a tactical lift system for inserting troops into combat. It was still a primitive machine, however, highly vulnerable to mechanical failure, carrying no armor and therefore threatened by even a single round from a light-caliber weapon. The art of vertical rescue was still new in 1950.

Colonel Pasqualicchio, after a harrowing crash landing where he suffered a fractured skull, undoubtedly didn't mind just how fragile his rescuer was as it came in to lift him out of a Korean rice paddy.

Colonel "Pancho" Pasqualicchio
18th Fighter Wing, 67th Fighter-Bomber Squadron

Shot Down and Picked Up

This was on April 19, 1951. The weather was sort of stinky at K-10, down at Chin Hae on the south coast. I made two mistakes that day. The squadron commander, Lieutenant Colonel Henry Lauris, asked for a volunteer for a mission, and I said, "I'll go with you, boss." The other mistake I made was that I had a waxed handlebar moustache, and I was getting sort of tired of tucking the spikes into my oxygen mask on every mission. So I snipped the spikes off, went on the mission, then promptly got shot down. From then on I never volunteered for another mission, and I never trimmed my moustache in combat for the next three hundred or so missions!

The mission that day was to go after a railroad tunnel on the railroad going into Sarawan, which was in the southwest portion of North Korea. On going up there—and all day long the weather was pretty stinky—we said, well, if we can't dive-bomb it, we'll skip-bomb it. We had 500-pounders with seven- to ten-second delay fuses on them. On the way up there, we were on top of the overcast. When we saw a hole, we went down below it and recognized the river. So, we flew up the river valley, approaching the target.

Now, we flew with the coolant switch in the manual position, so that if you took a hit in the coolant, the doors wouldn't open up to keep the engine cool and you'd detect a rise in your coolant temperature. [The P-51 had the distinctive bottom air scoop, located in the middle of the aircraft. The scoop had an automatic system that would open and close based on engine temperature. Most pilots kept the system on manual, since the doors would pop open the moment the flow of coolant dropped and precious seconds would pass before the pilot realized he had taken a critical hit.] As it turns out, I was hit by small-arms fire, probably just one .30-caliber slug, which went in beneath my left heel. I called my leader and said, "Boss, I think I'm hit. Check me." We didn't have a lot of room in that river valley, but we both did a 180-degree turn, and he said, "Roger, you're spewing coolant." So I said, "Get out of my way. I'm going to try to get rid of my bombs and my rockets and take this thing as far back as I can." After a short period of time—and we still had low cloud cover—the engine overheated, and soon it started torching. It was coughing and quitting, and I was running it on the primer for a little bit. Then she wouldn't run anymore, and I started losing altitude. I was too low to bail out, so I bellied into this rice paddy.

Just as I was bellying in, a dike appeared in front of me, and I caught the coolant scoop on the dike. In the process I fractured my skull and broke the airplane in half, though it stayed in pretty much one piece there in the paddy. There was still some torching going on in the engine, but the airplane didn't explode. The radio was working, so I called my boss to say that I was okay and to ask for help. Shortly after that, while I was standing on the ground beside my airplane, I saw a bunch of Koreans coming out from a nearby village.

My experience had been that when we had a guy down, if he tried to run into the woods to hide, you never saw him again. So I wanted to keep myself out in the open where my guys could protect me. Pretty soon, a couple of other 51s showed up. I had about half the air force covering me—in 51s, that is. Well, these Koreans came out of the village, and there were about seventy-five or so. None of them appeared to be very hostile, but I called my guys and said, "Put a burst of machine gun fire in front of them, but don't kill them. Just keep them away from me."

All but about three of them stayed back, and those three started walking toward the airplane. The 51s kept strafing, then called out, "What do you want us to do?" I said, "Let them come on through; I've got them covered with my .45." My .45 was shaking, because I was afraid. One of them came up to the airplane pretty close and was trying to tell me something, pointing toward the river. I couldn't understand him, and I was obviously scared. I guess after he saw my .45 waving around, he thought he'd better get out of there before I did some damage. He finally turned around and walked away.

One of my guys called me and said, "Hey, Panch, what did he want?" I said, "I don't know. They invited me to dinner, but since they're not having spaghetti, I said, 'No deal!' "

At that point, I just cooled my heels. My squadron leader had gone back to intercept the helicopter and escort him to my position. The helicopter was coming out of K-16, which was Yongdungpo. After about an hour or more on the ground, the helicopter showed up. Now, for several years I had seen these two red buttons in my P-51 that said PUSH TO DESTROY. That was on the old IFF [Identify Friend or Foe]. So, when the helicopter showed up, I pushed the buttons and nothing happened. I had expected a big explosion to occur.

About then the helicopter was on the ground, and the guys were yelling at me, "Come on! Come on!" I was standing there, shooting my .45 at my P-51 like a cavalryman would shoot his wounded horse! I managed to get into the helicopter, and we got away. They took me back to K-16, and it was dark when we landed, since this had been a late afternoon mission. A couple of the fighter pilots met me with a bottle of whiskey and some scrambled eggs.

Remarkably the fractured skull wasn't critical, though the bottle of whiskey most likely didn't help much. Recovering from his injuries, Pancho was back in the air and flying again in fairly short order. Apparently his adventure of getting shot down had not satiated his appetite for action, and when given the chance he and his flight leader slipped away for a "little fun" up north.

P-51s vs. MiGs

My flight leader, Bill Strand, and I were going on a mission together one day. We saw a pretty good target and got rid of our napalm. We sort of had it in the back of our minds that we'd like to go get us a MiG. He had already flown F-86s, and so had I, so we had our plans figured out. When we got rid of our napalm, we waltzed up to the Yalu River. By the time we got up there, Bill said, "You stay low, and I'll try to catch them at the top of their zoom."

So I was sitting there at about 6,000 or 8,000 feet, and he was up at about 16,000. All of a sudden, here I am, nose-to-nose with eight MiG 15s! I still had six rockets on my airplane, so I headed on into them. As I was approaching them, I pulled the nose up about 10 degrees and salvoed all six rockets into their faces. They scattered to the four winds, so I never saw the MiGs again, nor did Bill. But about that time, sixteen P-84s jumped me. Colonel Don Blakeslee was leading the 84s. One of his flight started to chase me around on the deck. They thought I was a Yak! Pretty soon, one of them recognized me as a P-51.

By the time I got home, I was summoned to Fifth Air Force Advance Headquarters in Seoul, where General Everest was commander. He chewed my tail out for a little bit in Blakeslee's presence. Then Blakeslee said, "You've screwed up this whole air war." When Blakeslee left, the general said, "Now, you stay the hell away from the Yalu River, and you just shoot at trucks.

Do you understand, Captain?" I said, "Yes, sir" and promptly left. I never did get into a tangle with any more MiGs, but we were anxious to grab a hold of any Yak or LA that we could get our hands on.

While in Korea, Pancho witnessed another rescue that left an indelible impression on him, not only due to the bravery of the downed pilot but for the display of compassion by an enemy soldier as well.

Bob Ward's Rescue from Behind the Lines

In April 1951, a young P-80 captain, Bob Ward, who was my roommate in the E&E [Escape and Evasion] training program, was shot down on the wrong side in the front lines. He broke one or both legs on ejection when his knees hit the windshield canopy bow. He was a tall, skinny jock, and he became a prisoner in the front-line "trenches." After a few days of diarrhea and pain from his broken legs, he tied two twigs together to form a cross. He thought he had had it. Well, one of his captors saw this and muttered "Christian." He befriended Ward and was designated to take him back to the rear area. In the middle of the night, he managed to let his truck run out of gas in the boonies and sent the two other guards to the next village for some petrol.

When they left he picked up Ward and carried him to the top of a hill. Bob didn't weigh very much after his stay behind the lines. After the Korean had set Bob down, he went back down to get the battery and one of the headlights from the truck. At this time, the B-26s were always going out on night missions, and appar-

ently this Korean recognized their standard routes.
Every time a B-26 would fly over, he'd flash it with the
headlight.

There was obviously a very alert Intelligence officer
doing debriefing when the 26s got home, because a
couple of them mentioned noticing the flashing of the
light. After the Intelligence officer heard this from a
couple of different pilots, he said, "Well, maybe there's
something up there. We need to go take a look tomorrow." So they sent a helicopter in with fighter escort
early in the morning. There they were, sitting on top of
the hill. The helicopter brought them both out. Bob
was a lucky guy, because he was so badly injured that
he couldn't walk.

7

SHOT DOWN

During the course of the Korean conflict approximately 250 airmen of the FEAF became prisoners of war of the North Koreans, Chinese, and secret Russian units operating in North Korea. Several more were shot down over Chinese territory, and though never officially listed, it's believed that one or more pilots might have been downed inside Soviet airspace.

The lot of a pilot downed in combat is a terrifying one. The experiences of World War II showed that even when flying against a belligerent who acknowledged the Geneva Convention treatment, if a pilot was captured survival was problematic. More than one American aircrew, falling into a German town they had been bombing but minutes before, met a swift and bloody end at the hands of enraged civilians.

The authors talked to one pilot, shot down by the Germans in 1944, who drifted straight down into the middle of a military compound. Several of the soldiers helped him out of his parachute, took his sidearm, and then offered him lunch while one of their officers discussed sports with him in English. The pilot quietly confessed to us that he was actually rather glad to have fallen straight into a German army unit, thus relieving him of the potential of being beaten to death by civilians just outside the military camp, a fate that nearly befell his crewmates, who had jumped out prior to him and had come down on the edge of a city they'd been tearing apart only minutes before.

Most pilots who bail out hit the ground dazed or in shock and are often wounded either by enemy fire or by the process of ejecting. Their transition is made more acute by the fact that in that fall to earth they have also fallen from one type of war into another. The war of a pilot is rarely personal. In air-to-air combat nearly every pilot describes it as going against another machine. There is a realization of kill or be killed, but the competition is professional in nature, a pitting of skills and training against a similar foe. It is also carried out wrapped inside the cocoon of a high-tech fighting machine and not crawling through the mud, gun or knife in hand.

The psychology of the fighter pilot is a key factor here as well. Highly trained, a combat pilot usually carries a bit of a gunslinger instinct of his superiority and aggressive spirit, as demonstrated by the likes of "Pancho" Pasqualicchio, who decided to cruise up to the Yalu in his Mustang with the sole intent of tangling with a MiG. Such an encounter has all the trappings of a medieval joust or a high-noon shootout rather than a brutal knife fight in a dark alleyway.

There is a supreme confidence in such a mentality that in most other settings would seem rather insane, but in the world of fighter pilots is perfectly understandable and acceptable. Pancho knew he was good, and he wanted to prove it the only way it could be proven, by bagging a jet while flying in a prop plane. The term "Hot Shot" was already in use. Any pilot worth his wings wanted to lay claim to that supreme accolade and there was only one way to get it: by going head-to-head with a MiG and coming out the winner.

This mentality is reinforced by the entire social caste system of the air force. During the Korean War hundreds of thousands of men and women served in the air force, but only a few thousand were the true "knights" of the air, going forth daily to joust with the knights wearing red armor. It was one thing to be in the air force; it was an entirely different thing to be a Hot Shot strapped into a P-51 or F-86. This was the one true way to prove that you indeed had the right stuff and belonged to the elite.

The entire realm of air combat was different as well, not just due to the jousting in the air but to all the aspects of air combat. Flak was a tracer of light flashing past or a silent black blossom, if too close followed by a sharp buffet. Ground targets were antlike hordes, toy trucks, occasionally an upturned face that when passed at 400 mph appeared as an indistinct blur.

There might be a few minutes of sweat-drenching fear as one raced into a flak-heavy target, or the glimpse of a tracer slashing from behind and a frantic warning from a wingman that someone was "on your six." Survive that moment, and twenty minutes later you were back on the flight line, leaning against the plane, joking with a crew chief as you pointed out a flak hole in the wing that slashed within inches of a fuel or hydraulic line. Then it was to debriefing, a good meal, and, if flying out of Japan, perhaps a night on the town.

But if the round that cracked through a fuselage nailed a coolant line, or tore open a fuel valve, and kerosene splashed uncontrolled against a red-hot turbine, everything changed in a matter of seconds. In a P-51 the hot smell of an engine burning up just inches from your legs filled the cockpit, or streams of oil cascaded over the forward windshield, instantly blocking out the world. If there was time you might give a quick call on the radio; if not you hoped a wingman did. There was usually the instant of worry that the canopy was clear, and if time allowed, a rolling of the plane onto its back, an unsnapping of harnesses, and a falling away.

In the newer jets with ejection systems, the first question as warning lights went on would be one of speed. With high-speed ejections, more than one pilot shattered his ankles, knees, or thighs as he blew clear. Eject when the plane was going too fast and you might wind up with a broken back or quite simply die.

In that instant the entire war for a pilot changed. Twenty minutes later he would not be on the tarmac, trading glib comments with anxious ground crews poking their fingers into holes, or putting on a bravado front with other pilots even though his back was still soaked with the sweat of fear.

Now he would see the world as those condemned to fight a war on the ground saw it. If fate was exceedingly cruel he'd float down onto the column of Chinese infantry he had been strafing only minutes before. Chances were he was dead before he even hit the ground; given the alternatives, it was usually a blessing if he was. Strafed infantry were rarely kind to the deliverer of such torment.

If he survived hitting the ground he'd suddenly be aware of all the elements outside of a cockpit. The stink of a Korean rice paddy in summer was often compared to falling into an outhouse, for the fertilizer in both was the same. If he had an open wound and was stuck out in the boonies for more than a day, it was an all but certain guarantee of a life-threatening infection, or, almost as bad, if he swallowed some of the water as he hit the paddy the results were all but certain to rush through him explosively in a matter of hours.

If it was winter, he would find himself experiencing a 100-degree shift in temperature in a split second. A winter ejection at high altitude could very well result in frostbite before he even reached the ground. If he ejected over the ocean, an immersion suit might keep him alive, but it was still a numbing experience. More than one pilot, after surviving all of that, would drown when he became tangled in his chute and was dragged under. Or in a high wind, the chute simply dragged him along like a sail, drowning him as well.

If a pilot did hit the ground and was capable of moving, training emphasized hiding the parachute, gaining cover, and trying to stay in contact until an evac unit came in. Given the high percentage of ejection injuries, or injuries from combat before bailing out, this was often an agonizing process of dragging a useless limb and struggling with shock. Then it was a matter of evasion and holding out.

The air force, in fact all air units in combat, demonstrated a fierce loyalty and protectiveness for any comrade forced down in enemy territory. The psychological impact of this effort was ofttimes crucial for the survival of the downed pilot. Lying numbed on the ground and still dazed from the landing, more than one pilot later testified that what revived him and gave him the strength to pick up the struggle was the sound of a comrade coming in at treetop level and then pulling into a tight protective circle, like a mother eagle hovering over a fallen chick.

Within minutes upwards of a dozen planes might be circling, laying down fire, strafing, and bombing to keep back enemy forces moving in for a capture. Overhead, pilots would scout out a safe lane of escape and fight to keep it open until the rescue chopper arrived.

The Chinese and Koreans, quick to adapt, soon figured out this aggressive stance toward the rescue of a downed pilot, and by the later part of the war trained their troops to turn it to their advantage. If command control could be maintained, encircling troops were often ordered to hold off contact. If time and terrain permitted, antiaircraft assets were positioned and the trap was laid. At what appeared to be the moment of rescue all hell would break loose, sometimes bringing down the chopper and protective aircraft circling low overhead. More than once these rescue attempts turned into bloody protracted battles with several pilots on the ground and dozens of aircraft vectoring in to beat the enemy back.

It is to the credit of the air force, navy, and marine rescue forces that never was a pilot abandoned when there was still a chance, no matter how remote, of getting him out. It was not just a cold-blooded realization on the part of the high command that such a commitment improved the morale of pilots going in harm's way, it was a personal understanding as well . . . a downed pilot was a comrade in need, and no man worthy of his wings would abandon a friend to the uncertain mercies of a ruthless foe.

★ ★ ★

One of the men who was not so lucky with pickup was Major James Kiser.

Major James Kiser
18th Fighter Group, 36th Squadron

Flying the F-80

I was initially trained in B-25s, went to the Philippines in 1949, and was assigned to the F-51 outfit, or P-51 in those days—the 18th Fighter Wing. I flew F-51s and later got checked out in F-80s before the war. That was a good airplane. I enjoyed it very much. You know, fighting the war wasn't all that much fun. Just a whole lot of moments of stark terror.

POW Experience

My capture is still very vivid in my mind. We were flying with a flight of four initially, and finally had to turn one of them back. We were going to Namsi, which we had been to several times before knocking out a railroad line from Sinuiju to Anju. There was a section of about 60 miles of road there that we kept cutting and trying to keep out of. On this day we were knocking out a bridge that was about four miles from the coast inland, bombing with 1,000-pound bombs with gun barrels screwed into the nose. (They screwed .50-caliber gun barrels into the nose of these bombs to make them stick good.)

I went down and dropped my bomb, and it just went off instantaneously, rather than waiting for the eight- to eleven-second delay fuse. In eight to eleven seconds, you have plenty of time to get away from the bomb. We were traveling 400 to 425 mph, and the blast took my left wing and blew me in an upward trajectory. The plane was rolling because of that blast on the left wing. I was on fire, since the blast also went into the cockpit.

I ejected, but my left foot had shrapnel in it and stayed on the pedal. My knee got chopped up on the canopy rings and the rail where the canopy joins the main part of the airplane there on the windshield. I didn't have much time, of course. I was only a few feet off the ground when I was hit. Going in an upward trajectory, I ejected and did not get out of my seat. My parachute had to come out around my shoulder harness, and therefore it did not get a full blossom at all. I just got a partial blossom. The seat kept me in a sitting position when I hit the backside of a pine forest. That saved me from a lot of glass shards and things, but I still picked up pine needles and splinters, and I was cut up pretty badly. But it saved me. My parachute caught in the trees enough to break my fall even at the speed I was traveling. It was just not my day.

When I got out of the seat, I could see that I was pretty badly hurt, but I had the presence of mind to wrap up my knee and my leg with part of my Mae West straps. Then I went back up on top of the hill I had just come down, and I had to use a stick to make a splint for my leg so that I could use my leg, which was kind of flapping both ways. When I got up there, I could see down below me toward the coast, and within about a half mile of me, a bunch of Korean soldiers were coming up the hill, shooting their guns and throwing hand grenades into the woods and the weeds. They didn't know where I was, I guess.

They kept coming on up the hill, so I went down toward them and hid behind a rock in a little crevice where I was covered with weeds. I could see them, but they couldn't see me unless they were right on me. I had one Korean come within just a few feet of me, and I followed him with my .45, but he never turned to look at me. That saved his hide and probably mine, too, because the rest of them would, of course, have killed me.

At any rate, I stayed there hidden, and they went on across the hill. This was late in the afternoon, and nightfall came very quickly. My wingman stayed for a long time, strafing the area near where I went down and where the troops had been, so he stirred them up quite a bit. But he didn't get home either. He ran out of gas on his way home and became a prisoner of war. I didn't know it until several months later, but he was captured and eventually put into the camp where I was kept for the rest of the war.

That night there came a real good rain, and I could hear some of the troops as they gradually came out of the woods. They'd be talking and coming by in pairs, and I thought most of them had pretty much gone, but I waited and I watched till after midnight before I made my move to start down. It was my intent to go west, down streams that I knew. I'd been to this area a number of times and all over it, so I knew the area. I headed to the coast where I knew there were some islands with some of our Korean agents positioned on them. They helped pick up troops if they got in a position to do it. So it was my intent to get there.

I saved my Mae West and everything as long as I could. As I was traveling out, I came on a Korean. I was kind of shocked at first. He charged me, and I got cut, but I was considerably larger than he was. I was able to overcome him and kill him.

I took his gun, his flashlight, and a bandolier of ammunition with me, then continued down from there. I kept following a stream until morning, when I started passing out. I was losing so much blood that I couldn't stay awake. I fell one time and awakened—I don't know how long I was out, but it was way up in the day—and I was in a rice paddy, submerged except for my head. I came very close to drowning in my sleep, but I was salvaged once more. I knew now that I was not going to be able to make it to the islands, so I thought, "Well, I need to find some kind of help if there's a way."

I found a Korean house that was out in the woods, kind of by itself, and I thought there might possibly be a sympathizer there that I might get some help from. So I sneaked up to the house as best I could and couldn't find anybody around. Korean huts have little mud kitchens that have a kind of a sunken area with a fire and a great big iron bowl that sits there that they cook their rice in, so I slipped down in there and found some kind of corn mush cooking. I stole some of that and I ate it before passing out again.

When I came to, there was a woman at the door, and she was carrying a baby and a load of firewood. She screamed, threw her baby and the firewood up in the air, and took off. I could hear that baby out there crying, but I couldn't get up, so I just pulled out my .45 again. I thought I was probably going to be killed, but I passed out again. The next thing I remember, I was out in a courtyard and stripped. All my clothes were gone, and they'd taken my weapon and everything I had.

I was a prisoner.

The next several weeks I spent as the personal prisoner of a bunch of Koreans. They'd drum up a crowd, and I'd get tied up in the middle of the village, and they'd invite everybody. Everyone would come over and beat me with sticks. One woman even brought her baby over there and let him urinate all over me. An old man came down—an old gray-haired man with a long, gray beard and a funny-looking hat—he came down the hill as I was lying there helpless, unable to do anything, and he just beat the tar out of me with that stick. Well, that was just the start of several weeks of that kind of treatment.

This went on for I don't know how many weeks—several weeks—and then a band of Chinese came through and took me as their prisoner. Then I started getting some English treatment. I mean they could speak English enough to ask me some questions. They wanted me to tell them where I came from, but name, rank and, serial number was all I would give them until they got to the point where they wanted me to sign letters and things like that saying that I was wrong for being in Korea.

I said, "You know I can't do that. There's no way that I can do it. You'll just have to shoot me."

I was the only prisoner they had for a long time. Then a bomber crew came in. A B-29 had been shot down not too far from us. The crew and I became close friends. The co-pilot had been killed, along with a couple of others, but the main part of that crew was with me then for the rest of the war. We ended up going back into the camp area eventually. It was in August that I went down, but I didn't get into a camp until December. We were then taken north all the way into around the Pyongyang and Sunan area. I didn't get beaten anymore. But as far as following the rules went, I'm not sure their rules were the same that we all felt were proper rules for prisoners. It was a different kind of war. They attempted initially to brainwash us into becoming Communists or something. They wanted us to listen to lectures—readings from Marx and Lenin and things of that sort. They had all kinds of material like that that they wanted us to read.

It became a farce in many cases, because they wanted one of our people to read aloud, and they would leave us under the guard of soldiers who couldn't understand English! Some of our guys who were really smart would stand up with a book in front of them and tell jokes, and we'd laugh. But when we'd laugh, we'd be in trouble. Some of our guys had the gift of gab and were real good at these "readings," so it became a wonderful farce. The Koreans thought they were brainwashing us, I guess. Here the temperature was way below zero, we didn't have any clothes, and we were freezing to death—yet they wanted us to sit in there and listen to them reading from Marx and Lenin.

Major Kiser was one of the fortunate ones. He survived the beatings, brainwashing, and lack of food and proper medical treatment, and when the armistice was signed he was repatriated. Thirty-five of his comrades, known to be in captivity at the end of the war, never returned. Since the collapse of the Soviet empire, reports have surfaced that a number of pilots thought to have unique technical knowledge, or sometimes for no apparent reason at all, were shipped to Russia.

In Russia these gallant men endured months and sometimes years of unrelenting interrogations, torment, and brainwashing. The realization was undoubtedly there as well that all hope of rescue was gone forever . . . they had been abandoned by the country they had volunteered to serve. Families would be informed that they were dead, spouses would remarry, children would grow up never knowing that their father was still alive and languishing in a prison on the other side of the world.

There are indications that some of these men survived for years in the Soviet gulag until they finally died from maltreatment or were "disposed of" when it was felt they were no longer of use. There are indications that our government was aware of this "transfer," but no public efforts were ever mounted to gain their release.

It is clear that the same thing happened again twenty years later in Vietnam with reports that a number of our pilots were left behind after that "peace" agreement as well. There are dark reports that some of these abandoned men might then have been removed to China and perhaps Russia, too.

May it never happen again.

8

A NEW KIND OF WAR

Korea was a war of elusive and constantly shifting goals. When the conflict started in June 1950, American forces were caught completely unawares and driven back in headlong retreat. For the first several weeks of the conflict, it was simply a question of could we even maintain a presence on the peninsula or would we be forced into a Dunkirk withdrawal? It was a situation perhaps even more desperate than the Battle of the Bulge.

No matter how desperate that struggle was, there had been an understanding that even though we'd been caught by surprise, ultimately the outcome would be ours. The American combat infantry caught in the Ardennes quickly rose to the occasion. In short order, General Patton had begun his famous flanking maneuver from the South, and all that was needed was a break in the weather to bring in our overwhelming air assets.

Hard as it might sound, even if Bastogne and the 101st Airborne had been lost, it was doubtful that the Nazi juggernaut would ever have reached Antwerp.

Even if it had, the inevitable tide of the war would have continued forward. Within a week of the start of the German offensive, men such as Patton and Bradley were beginning to see it as a suicidal throwing away of the remaining German armor and heavy infantry reserves, and the Bulge could be converted into a cauldron annihilating the German army on the western front.

Six years later in Korea, the weeks of retreat southward were just that, a full-blown retreat. The vast majority of American troops in the theater were not veterans of Normandy and the race across France but, rather, postwar draftees, poorly trained, lightly equipped, and completely unprepared for a brutal fighting withdrawal in primitive conditions. It is a testament to their innate skills and pride as Americans that they rose to the occasion and fought successfully to create a last-stand lodgment around Pusan in the southeast corner of Korea.

Thus ended the first defensive stage of the conflict. MacArthur's bold step at Inchon opened the second stage, though even here the strategic goal was initially limited in scope with the mission of flanking the North Korean army in the South and liberating the country. The victorious enemies of June were now in headlong retreat themselves by September.

The third step was the decision in late September to cross the border into North Korea in hot pursuit and to finish off the aggressor army. The issue of Chinese and even Russian intervention was dismissed as of little consequence, and as discussed earlier, the heat of action and the nature of the North Korean aggression all but eliminated any prospect of a negotiated settlement at this point. Invasion northward, if need be all the way to the Yalu, was all but a foregone conclusion.

According to many with a pro-airpower leaning, this move northward to a large extent ignored the true operational situation relative to logistics and airpower. One of the reasons for the rapid collapse of North Korean forces was that as they advanced deep into South Korea, their logistical support lines were stretched for hundreds of miles and thus extremely vulnerable to interdiction from the air.

As the Koreans retreated into the North, the reverse now became true: their lines accordioned shut, as demonstrated by the eventual withdrawal of some of the B-29 forces due to lack of targets. The official air force history of the conflict argues that perhaps too much emphasis was placed on the ground offensive as a result of Inchon, and not enough on the fact that logistically the Koreans had already shot their bolt and were on the point of collapse. Following this logic, the air force believes that few truly realized that as the Koreans withdrew they were, in fact, like a coiled spring, compressing and thus gaining in power for a counterstrike, through the massive assistance of the Chinese.

Stage four was one of confusion as to ultimate objectives and threats. Were the Chinese going to intervene; should the war now be one of unification, this time under a pro-Western government based in the South; should it be punitive only and once the North Koreans came to the table, troops would be withdrawn to the 38th parallel; or, as some hawks argued, should it simply keep on pushing, perhaps even with the intent of going over the Yalu and wiping out sanctuaries on the far side of that river?

These questions were never really answered as stage five began, the debacle of yet another withdrawal, this one in many ways even more fraught with peril than the counterattack of the previous summer. Again it was a fight for survival rather than a drive toward victory and a bringing of the boys home by Christmas.

As the spring of 1951 progressed, United Nations forces slowly forced their way back through Seoul and a score of miles north beyond the 38th parallel. And then the entire complexion of the war changed . . . with the beginning of armistice talks at Kaesong.

For the American military, this was a situation all but unique in its history: to be actively involved in combat involving hundreds of thousands of men, and sustaining thousands of casualties, while at the same time openly negotiating for an armistice that could literally be signed at any moment, but in fact would drag on for two more years.

For most European and Asian powers, this was an old game, but it went against the grain of the American military tradition. After the victory at Yorktown in the fall of 1781, the Revolution did, in fact, drag on for two more years. Negotiations with Britain did open the following year, but at the same time military operations in North America wound down, with Washington disengaging and withdrawing to Newburgh, 50 miles north of New York, to wait out the talks.

During the Civil War, the Confederate government did attempt to negotiate a settlement, but the meeting lasted for only several days and quickly came to naught, since Lincoln clearly saw total victory was only weeks away. It was in that war as well that the American military tradition of fighting an unlimited war to total unconditional surrender was clearly established. Combat was to be unrelenting until the enemy collapsed (and then we would rebuild them).

The manner in which World War I ended, through

an armistice that did not bring with it the sense of total victory, quickly triggered a reaction in our nation and contributed in no small way to the isolationism that followed. It clearly influenced our approach to World War II that anything less than total victory was unacceptable.

It was calling for a complete readjustment of mindset for troops, especially drafted troops, to accept the idea that they could be called upon to die, only to then suffer the horrible irony of falling or being crippled just hours before an armistice was reached.

It became evident from the start, too, that the Red Chinese and North Koreans saw the negotiations in a different light than the westerners facing them across the table. Americans have always maintained, perhaps too idealistically, the belief that war is an aberration in the orderly process of relationships between nations. There is peace, and then the stepping off into a dark abyss called war that should be crossed as quickly as possible.

Mao perceived war and peace as a single continuum, an integrated process one traveled upon, flowing from one position to the other at will, in order to achieve an ultimate goal. The two were interchangeable and in fact complemented each other. The Reds therefore approached the negotiating table as simply a means of achieving a given goal, of which one aspect was gaining the advantage on the battlefield by the weakening of resolve and ideally by the splitting of wills among the various United Nations forces.

There was an additional gear hidden within the machinery of this war . . . Joseph Stalin. For the Soviets there was everything to be gained and little to lose by the continuation of the conflict. After the removal of MacArthur it was quite evident that all will was gone for a significant widening of the war. Knowing this, a dragging out of the conflict for an indeterminable period could only serve the Soviet Union.

Significant American resources were being diverted to Korea and chewed up. Every tank, plane, truck, and soldier sent into that conflict was one less deployed to Europe. It was a perfect lab to observe American military techniques and to test equipment, especially aircraft, head-to-head. Finally there was the Machiavellian aspect: though China was now supposedly in the Communist camp, it was still a traditional foe of the Russian empire. Tying Mao's forces down in Korea was an excellent way of keeping him diverted from other concerns. Many historians now believe that it was no simple coincidence that the peace talks were fruitless until the death of Stalin on March 5, 1953. Four months later the war was over.

The alleged peace talks would hang over the conflict for the next two years, raise profound questions at home regarding the nature of the war, affect a presidential election, and plant in the back of the mind of every United States combatant the lingering question of what it was we were indeed fighting for and what result we were seeking if not total victory. Peace without total victory was a harsh new reality of the Cold War era.

This was compounded by the startling removal of General MacArthur as Supreme Commander on April 11, 1951.

In a war filled with controversy, this incident stands as one of the most controversial. General MacArthur is a hero straight out of a Greek tragedy, filled with greatness yet also one trapped by fatal flaws. His landing at Inchon was an audacious move, demonstrating

strategic brilliance, the same as his campaign in the
southern Pacific in 1942–1943. His insightful understanding of the nature of the Japanese people, and his
shogunlike postwar-reconstruction management, were
so influential that a serious petition was actually presented to him by a group of Japanese delegates beg-
ging for the right to join the United States.

It was his ego and a supreme sense of confidence,
his belief that he alone could truly grasp the route to
victory, that brought about his eventual downfall.
Whether he was right or not in what he demanded is
still a topic open to debate.

It's important to remember the overall paradigm of
politics in the Far East in order to grasp the complex-
ity of what was happening in Korea in the winter of
1950–1951. The last Nationalist forces had withdrawn
from the mainland only the year before and a de facto
state of war still existed between the two sides. American naval forces patrolling the straits between Formosa and the mainland were all that kept the two
belligerents apart. The Nationalists openly declared
that the withdrawal was but a temporary one and once
their forces were properly rebuilt and rearmed, the
struggle would be launched anew.

In the same year that the Nationalists retreated,
America was shocked to discover that its monopoly on
atomic weapons had been wiped away by the Soviet
detonation of an atomic bomb. With the rapid reduc-
tion in American military forces in the immediate
postwar years, the reliance on the atomic trump card
was the cornerstone of our policy of military contain-
ment of Russia. It had been safely assumed that it
would be at least ten or more years before the Soviets
achieved atomic capability, so no matter what their

ground troop strength they would never dare to act against our national interests.

The collapse of China also meant that its use as a counterforce to Soviet expansion in the East was finished, and in fact this new alignment presented a profound threat to the entire region. It was fully realized that any actions by China at this stage would in fact be a proxy service to Soviet intentions and would be backed by Stalin, who now had a growing arsenal of atomic weapons.

On November 28, 1950, MacArthur openly acknowledged that a significant number of Chinese troops were now arrayed against United Nations forces in Korea, though for the next several days he still maintained that the enemy offensive could be contained north of Pyongyang. Less than a week later, though, he acknowledged to the Joint Chiefs that the situation was far graver than originally believed. He also declared his belief that the United Nations was facing the full strength of Red China in an undeclared war by that nation and that it was time to make "political decisions and strategic plans . . . adequate fully to meet the realities involved."

The immediate reply from the Joint Chiefs, conveying the opinion of President Truman, was that the primary objective for MacArthur at this juncture was simply to preserve his troops and prevent their destruction. The holding of territory so far conquered or the full destruction of the enemy capability to wage war was not the main goal of the operation.

Early in the struggle Chiang Kai-shek had offered over 30,000 "volunteers" out of his Nationalist forces to fight in the defense of Korea. That offer had been rejected, at least on the surface, with the statement

that such a move might reduce the defenses of Formosa to a dangerous level. In reality there was grave
concern that Nationalist Chinese fighting in Korea
might very well trigger a Red Chinese intervention.
Now that Red China was in the war, MacArthur
pressed for the release of Nationalists for use on the
peninsula. In addition, however, he proposed a far
broader commitment on the part of Formosa.

With his statement that the United Nations was
truly engaged in a full-scale war with China he questioned the reasoning for limiting such operations to
Korea, citing among other reasons the obvious fact
that Chinese aircraft were operating out of airfields
north of the Yalu, and that in the first weeks of the expanded conflict we had so far conceded to the enemy
the right of maintaining a safe haven.

MacArthur called for the release of Nationalist
forces and the providing of amphibious and air support, allowing Chiang to strike along the coast of
China while at the same time the American navy
would institute a blockade of Chinese ports and bom-
bard targets on the mainland as well. This would force
Mao to redistribute his ground forces to defend thousands of miles of coastline.

In addition, air attacks should start at once, not only
against airfields north of the Yalu, but also against
troop concentrations, transport, and industrial infrastructure supporting the Chinese war effort.

These statements, along with a statement from the
president on November 30 declaring that the United
Nations should reserve to itself whatever means necessary to bring about a military solution in Korea, sent
a ripple through the global community.

England, among others, expressed immediate concern, especially over the veiled implication concerning the use of atomic weapons in the president's November 30 statement to take all means necessary to defend United Nations forces already in Korea. Truman quickly rephrased his words, and the State Department soon made an outright statement eliminating contemplation of the bombing of Manchuria as a response that would threaten to widen the war into a general Asian conflict.

There were other concerns besides political ones tied into this decision. The Berlin crisis of 1948 and the explosion of a Soviet atomic bomb in 1949 served as the impetus for a renewed buildup of American strategic assets. The B-29, though still formidable, was beginning to show its age, and though an upgraded version, the B-50, was in service the number available was limited. The largest bomber ever built by the United States, the B-36, had to be reserved for the potential mission of striking at Russia, therefore the means to actually deliver a full-scale strategic bombardment of China and sustain it for the long haul was problematic. The only way it was seen to engage in such an operation was to gut out those squadrons dedicated to serving as a counterforce to the Soviet Union, and it could be fairly assumed that until aircraft production was significantly geared up, losses would quickly reduce our capability even further. In short, the mighty American war machine of 1945, which could put thousands of bombers into the air simultaneously and at opposite ends of the world, was simply no longer there.

Finally there was the true root cause of concern: the Soviet Union. Even if the industrial capacity of Manchuria was significantly reduced, it would do nothing to halt the flow of supplies out of Russia. In fact, such a

campaign, even if Russia did not become directly involved, might actually serve to strengthen the Soviet
position by devouring our air assets and thus reducing
the threat to Russia if it should decide to act elsewhere, such as in Europe. Beyond that, though, was the
far larger concern, that of a full-scale war in Asia.

If America should indeed find itself drawn into a
large-scale Asian conflict, it would be forced to fight
such a conflict 7,000 miles from home, with a gargan-
tuan logistical tail, while China and Russia could
throw millions of troops into the struggle and thousands upon thousands of aircraft.

This, then, was the crux of the argument among
MacArthur, the Joint Chiefs, the State Department,
and the president. Could America accept the concept
of a limited war? At the same time could we accept
the paradigm of allowing our enemies to decide arbi-
trarily how and when the war could be expanded, limited, or reduced?

The controversy raged through the winter while the
fighting dragged on. A Chinese special delegation to the
United Nations declared itself to be disassociated from
the "volunteers" fighting in Korea and insisted that if
there was to be a ceasefire all "aggressor" forces had to
leave the peninsula, and that in addition America had to
pull its forces out of the Formosa region as well, a demand that was clearly impossible to accept.

The message, however, was clear from our allies,
the United Nations, and then finally from the president, that even though the Chinese were using bases
outside of Korea, the action had to be limited to Korea. The Russians added a pointed remark that sent
shivers through many, that America was using Japan
as a base of operations, a situation analogous to China.
The threat there was clear.

It was this continued debate between a total war fought to win and a limited war for limited objectives, which at this point was simply to reestablish a prewar status quo, that finally drove an irreconcilable wedge between the president and MacArthur, the Supreme Commander, United Nations Forces. The debate finally went public, and on April 11, 1951, Truman received MacArthur's resignation.

The old warrior, representing warfare from a different age, faded from the scene, to be replaced by General Matthew B. Ridgway. In that spring and summer, the nature of the war in Korea changed and with it the entire reality of warfare for America from that time up to the present day. The era of total war, of black and white, of pursuit to a truly final and ultimate victory was gone forever; it was now a realm of twilight struggles fought to a gray conclusion.

For the pilots in Korea, the day-to-day operations remained the same, bombing, strafing, tangling with the Chinese over the Yalu, or "MiG Alley," as it was now called. This new kind of struggle brought with it as well the need for a higher professionalism, a willingness to go forth and, if need be, die in a struggle that had no true absolutes . . . and the Hot Shots rose to the occasion.

9

THE NEW PARADIGM

As the ground war finally stalled into a stalemate just north of the 38th parallel, the air force was there in earnest, providing three basic types of missions.

The first was direct tactical support on the battlefield. Called in at a moment's notice, and still flown primarily by P-51s, these attack missions helped to throw back the Chinese human wave assaults, soften up enemy positions, and provide top cover for United Nations troops. Over this part of the battlefield, the United States Air Force ruled virtually unopposed, with only rare hit-and-run strikes by Korean and Chinese air units. In one remarkable throwback to World War I, the North Koreans actually sent up ancient biplanes for night attacks, the small aircraft usually cruising up high over their own lines, shutting down their motors, then drifting in over allied lines to drop hand grenades and mortar rounds.

The second basic type of mission was supply interdiction between the front lines up to the Yalu River. Main targets were fixed positions, such as railroad lines, bridges, tunnels, docks, and industrial facilities. These targets were at times death traps, heavily ringed with flak and occasionally defended by air units as well. Given the mountainous terrain, strike forces would sometimes face the unenviable task of going into a target with flak firing down on them from above. Along these routes the Chinese sustained tens of thousands of casualties as they moved troops, usually by foot, from the Yalu down to the front. Companies, battalions, sometimes even entire divisions, would lose more than half their men if they were caught in the open.

The third basic mission was that of air superiority, the arena for this action, MiG Alley, the airspace along the Yalu River basin. It should be remembered that in this new jet age, a high-flying fighter could literally traverse all of Korea in a matter of minutes or sweep from China down to the 38th parallel in a little more than a half hour. Unless air cover was set to interdict Chinese strikes, aircraft engaging in interdiction raids or providing support directly over the battlefield were vulnerable. Thus it was essential to set up a line of defense as far north as possible to block Chinese access into Korea.

During the spring of 1951 the Chinese air force went through a massive buildup as the Soviet Union shipped hundreds of aircraft, complete with ground crews and instructors, into Manchuria in a display of socialist brotherhood. Overnight the Chinese air force was transformed into a combat force that actually outnumbered the American jet assets in the Far East. Estimates are that by the middle of the summer the Chinese were capable of putting more than four hundred MiGs into the air, *at one time*! In response, during the early summer of 1951, there were less than a hundred Sabres available, with air bases more than 200 miles away, compared to 20 miles for the Reds.

Staging out of China, hundreds of MiGs were poised to rise up and give battle or refuse action altogether if their commanders felt that the odds weren't right. Thus the Hot Shots heading north might face days of patrolling empty airspace, and then suddenly without warning find themselves in a tangle with a dozen or more MiGs.

Colonel Ralph Parr with the 18th received his initiation to MiG Alley early in June 1951.

Colonel Ralph Parr (double ace)
18th Fighter Wing

First Encounter

I had a pair of flying gloves—which you were supposed to wear—only because I brought them with me. I had a flying suit only because I brought *it* with me. I was wearing a broken jet helmet that was held together by masking tape. I had a couple of guys in my flight that were flying with plastic football helmets on, because we didn't have helmets. That's how it was when I first started flying in Korea.

It was the end of May, and I wanted to get checked out and flying air-to-air combat, which is what I'd always wanted to do since I was knee-high to a grasshopper. I finally got scheduled to go up there [to the Yalu], and that particular mission happened to me on the seventh of June.

I was flying number 4 position. The flight leader was leading a four-ship flight, and we were a combat air patrol. We cruised up the Yalu River on our side of it, and

since I was the number 4 position, I took my positioning off my number three man, who was my leader—an
element leader, at least.

I was in a position where I was looking across the
other airplanes and watching their tails and also looking across the river. There wasn't a cloud in the sky. It
was just as clear as a bell. In fact, if we could have gone
up a little higher we'd have probably seen Europe.

All of a sudden I saw four MiGs coming down about
90 degrees to us—straight into us. They were all firing,
so I called a break, and my flight leader broke the
wrong way. However, at the time he broke, the MiGs
weren't even trying to turn with us, so he just pressed
on. By the time he got turned around, even though he'd
turned the same way, they had overshot (keeping their
speed up) and climbed back up and out of sight. We
were up at about 44,000 feet.

When we finished the break, it left us with two elements of two up there. My element had gone in the
right direction and the other hadn't, and we had flown
apart at about 600 miles an hour. It doesn't take too
long to be several counties away from each other. You
can't find each other; you can't see each other.

Now, the enemy was starting to fly larger formations
up there. So the rules for that week and that particular
day were that if you got broken down below four ships,
start withdrawing and come home. So we had turned
around and were headed south down the Yalu. Earlier,
my element leader had made the comment as we were
walking out to the airplane: "You know, you've got a
lot more 86 time than I do. If you see something up
there, and I can't see it right away, I'll clear you to take
it. I'll cover you." So I quietly thought to myself, "That
sounds like a good deal." He was a second lieutenant

and a "shiny" pilot, but he didn't have a very deep background of experience. And I did. I had more F-86 time than he had total time.

As we cruised down toward the mouth of the Yalu River, I was looking all over the place, having already seen the front end of four enemy airplanes up close. I was pretty alert at the time—had a lot of adrenaline flowing. I looked down and I saw a movement flicker across a little yellow patch down there—probably a little patch of sand next to the river—and it was driving right toward me. And we were now at 41,000 feet, having lost 3,000 feet in the break, and we were starting to bleed our way back up but hadn't really gotten back up yet.

So I called it out, and he looked down there and he couldn't see it. Well, I couldn't see it then either, but I knew roughly where it was headed. So he says, "Roger. You take it. I've got you covered."

So I rolled up—actually I rolled over—and I threw my speed brakes in. I had 100 percent power on, and I could almost look over the nose and see behind me. I was going straight down.

My wingman called me and said, "Which way did you go?" I said, "I went straight down," and I gave him the heading that I was starting to pull out on. I said, "Come on down and see if you can find me." He said, "Okay."

I started to pull out. I looked at my altimeter, which had a built-in lag past 10,000 feet. Now, the good book on flying the airplane says you need at least 14,500 feet for a pullout if you're at .92 Mach. And I was up around Mach 1. I'd already passed 10,000, so I started a pretty strong pullout.

You wind up gritting your teeth, holding your breath and tightening up all your muscles, and pinching your neck down to keep all the blood from running out your brain. Slowly but surely the nose came up. I had to increase the Gs up to around seven or eight. And you can't breathe with that G suit filling your lungs.

I came out at about two or three hundred feet. The airplane was flying very uncoordinated, because it was beyond its limiting Mach number. I kept looking up front and looking up front, and I picked out a flight of two—whoops!—that was a flight of four, no, six, no, a flight of eight!

I thought, "Hell, they're talking about the peace treaty being signed any day now, so why not?" I decided to go up and take the leader, because I figured he had more experience than the guys he was leading. About that time, I glanced off to the right and the left, and over on my left side sat eight more of them!

So there were sixteen of them down there—just about a squadron strength. Well, I went churning in there and, just as I was about to shoot at the leader, the other flight saw me, called me out, and broke real fast. Like chucking a banana into a high-speed fan, they went in every direction except down. I was still going so fast that I was having trouble controlling the airplane. I pulled up and followed the leader in the break, got him in about a 70- or 80-degree deflection shot, and I hit him. But when I pulled the trigger, I had nine and a half Gs on the airplane. I wasn't aware of it until that moment, but the electric motors wouldn't raise the ammunition to the guns at that many Gs, so the guns immediately started to slow down.

I got off the trigger before they stopped. But the fuse in the gunsight blew, because it wasn't braced to stand that many Gs. So I didn't have any gunsight now. I slid up alongside of the lead, and he had started a roll. I was a little behind him in the roll.

What we had, basically, were two airplanes flying almost canopy-to-canopy, doing rolls at very low altitude and staying within not quite wingtip clearance of each other. This went on for I don't know how many rolls. When I looked straight up out of the cockpit, I could see the pilot's feet on the floor of his cockpit. Something happened—I don't know what it was—but I got a very slight advantage on him. I crossed the controls, threw my speed brakes out, and it made him ease forward a little bit.

When he saw he couldn't stop it, he went ahead and threw the throttle into it, so I threw the throttle to mine. I had been there in idle power trying to stay behind him. So, when I punched the throttle and slid in behind him, I thought I was going to hit his tail. If I had opened the canopy and just leaned forward, I think I could have touched it!

I was waiting to hear metal grind as I went down the back edge of his horizontal stabilizer. But when my wingtip went into his jetwash, it punched me back about five to eight feet, and now I was sitting about ten or fifteen feet behind him. So I put a good burst into him, but he wasn't sitting still. He was maneuvering that airplane for all he was worth.

Every time I pulled the trigger, the vibration of the guns would stall my airplane. I worked my way back up about four or five times, and the last time it was like somebody had thrown ten gallons of water into my face—into the airplane. I guess I had hit one of his fuel tanks, which dumped a whole bunch of fuel on me. And the last time I got back up there and pulled the trigger on him, he caught fire.

Then the fire came back, went over the top of my canopy, over both sides of the fuselage, and all the way back around the tail. He just loomed up real fast in front of me, and I broke away to keep from ramming him. I looked around real quick to see if there was anybody else, and there were seven more MiGs down there. Apparently eight of the sixteen MiGs had pulled up and covered the fight, and the other eight stayed down there to fight me. And my wingman was still trying to find me!

When the leader burst into flames on the ground, my wingman spotted that and kept calling out, "What's your position?" The only thing I would say back to him was, "Don't bother me. I'm busy!" I only have a vague memory of answering him, and he laughed about it later. "Yeah," he said, "there you were down there with eight of 'em, and you were dancing with 'em!"

Tactics

"Boots" Blesse and I came back after our first tour in Korea and got in the same outfit in the States that was flying F-86s. We used to go out daily and just break our heads on each other, trying to figure out different maneuvers—where one airplane could get an advantage over another.

We didn't know *what* our tactics were at the time—we just figured them out as we went along. But Boots finally got them all down on paper [*No Guts, No Glory*], and he got reassigned to Korea and made ten kills—so obviously we were doing something right!

We practiced high-speed barrel rolls, low- and high-speed yo-yos, vertical reverses, plus anything that popped up when an opening showed itself. When you're talking air-to-air combat tactics and maneuvers, it's sort of like a game of chess. You have got to—in

your own mind—be about three or four moves ahead
of the other guy. When you do something, you know
he's watching you, and you know what he's going to
try to do when he sees you start to do something. So
you lead him into that to get him to commit himself,
and then you do something else. If you train for the
worst scenario, the best scenario will take care of itself.

Korea did teach us a lot but, unfortunately, there was
enough space between Korea and Vietnam that most of
the people who learned the lessons were not available—they had retired.

On July 27, 1953, Colonel Parr was again on duty over
North Korea, on what was already known to be the
last day of the war, announcement of the armistice
having just been released. Escorting a recon flight,
their job was to get a final look around, particularly at
North Korean airfields, to try to get a final count so
that if any reinforcements came in after the ceasefire
it would be noted.

None of the MiGs ventured up to offer a challenge.
Just as the recon plane turned to head back south,
Parr spotted a transport plane flying down near the
surface. The war was still officially on. Parr dived in
for the kill, swung in on the transport's six, and
dropped it. It was the last air-to-air kill of the war.

The transport was Colonel Parr's tenth victory,
ranking him along with Colonel James Johnson and
Colonel Harold Fischer as sixth ranking ace of the
war.

10

1951: THE LONG WAR BEGINS

With the start of the peace talks at Kaesong (later that year they would move to Panmunjom), the war settled down into a waiting game, one that the Chinese suspected they could turn to their advantage.

Their own plans had called for a renewal of offensive operations in the spring, the "Big Red Attack," as it was called by Radio Pyongyang. The stated goal was the elimination of United Nations forces in Korea.

Even before the offensive started in the last week of April 1951, ceaseless interdictions from the Yalu down to the front were destroying vast quantities of supplies throughout the winter. The Chinese found they could maintain a strong holding operation with local offensive strikes, but anything much beyond that was out of the question; thus the buildup for the April attacks was a logistical nightmare for the Red forces.

Like Germany in 1944–1945, the strategic air war in and of itself did not bring the enemy to their knees, but it made it difficult to move and destroyed vast quantities of war materiel long before it ever reached the front. Chinese units unfortunate enough to get caught in the open by an air strike would often be torn to ribbons, losing hundreds of men in a matter of minutes.

On the night of April 22, 1951, the Chinese kicked off their offensive with well over 300,000 men. From the start, United Nations air units were flying round the clock sorties, usually well over a thousand a day, to break up the attack.

For example, on April 23, 1951, two F-80 Shooting Stars were vectored in on a company of Chinese soldiers near the Imjin River. Equipped with fragmentation bombs armed with proximity fuses, the jets were deadly, often falling upon their target before the enemy were even aware they had been spotted. They plastered the unit with half a ton of air-burst fragmentation bombs, then strafed mercilessly. The company was annihilated in a matter of minutes. On that first day of the attack, the Fifth Air Force inflicted nearly 2,000 casualties on enemy forces.

On the ground, allied strategy was to fall back slowly to preprepared positions, to spare the lives of troops, and to call in a firestorm of artillery and air strikes. The unrelenting Chinese attacks finally drove United Nations forces yet again into the suburbs of Seoul.

Task Force 77 moved three carriers into the fight to provide additional support, adding nearly 300 aircraft to the fight. On April 27, the air force caught an estimated 6,000 Chinese troops ferrying across the Han River in an attempt to outflank Seoul. When the air strikes were finished, the few survivors were mopped up by Republic of Korea Marines.

B-29s were pressed into night attacks. Each bomber carried forty 500-pound fragmentation bombs with proximity fuses. Bursting over the target, each bomb showered an area of half an acre with a numbing

15,000 splinters. Near Inje, on the eastern front, an ROK unit called in a single B-29 after being driven off a crucial hilltop position. The following morning they easily retook the hill and counted over 800 Chinese dead, with clear indications that hundreds of wounded had been dragged away during the night. Chinese POWs expressed outright terror of these nighttime saturation attacks. In another attack, an American soldier, who had been taken prisoner earlier in the day, reported surviving a terrifying night strike that killed hundreds and triggered a panic. In the confusion he was able to slip away and regain friendly lines.

Near Chunchon a recon flight reported an entire battalion of enemy troops moving into a tunnel. Napalm was dropped at both ends and then HE was used to seal the entryways. Night attacks of upwards of eighty B-29s plastered division-size areas with airburst fragmentation bombs while unrelenting day strikes continued the punishment. If ever in the history of warfare there stands an argument for the power of air units to directly influence a ground war, it is in the turning back of the Chinese spring offensive.

By the end of May, the attacks had petered out. Tens of thousands of enemy troops were dead and wounded, tens of thousands of tons of supplies destroyed. Every plane available to the United Nations air forces flew straight out for over two months and turned the tide. It was out of this debacle that the Communists' decision to go to the negotiating table formed when their high command realized that dislodging UN forces from Korea by military means was impossible. The United States Air Force had made the difference.

★ ★ ★

The P-51 was still in the fight. Given its evolution into a ground support aircraft, it is interesting to consider the original intent of the plane's designers. Designated as the A-36, it was planned to serve as a dive bomber and fighter-bomber. It was the British who mated the frame to the famous Merlin engine, added the four-blade prop, and set it on the path as the most famous of the Allied air-superiority weapons of World War II.

Some of the veterans of that conflict feel that the old P-47 Thunderbolt, or "Jug" as it was affectionately referred to by those who flew it, was by far the better plane. More than one veteran, when describing a close call in their 47, declared that if they had been in a Mustang they would have been dead. The Jug could take tremendous punishment and keep right on flying; the Mustang was far more vulnerable, especially if a shot hit a coolant line (the P-47 was air cooled). A few cynics even point out that at approximately $50,000, the Mustang cost only a quarter of a P-47's price tag, and that this was a big motivator as well for the government to adopt the plane. Of course, there is one key point that serves as a counterbalance: the P-51 was a flying gas can, with far lower fuel consumption than a 47, and it could range all the way to Berlin and return.

Its lighter frame and coolant system did indeed make it vulnerable to ground fire, and thus a ground strike mission was far more harrowing for pilots, many of them undoubtedly wishing they were in a Jug or, better yet, a Russian Stormovik, an aircraft specifically designed to fly into a hail of fire and come out the other side with the engine still running and the pilot still in one piece.

By 1950, however, the Jug was a thing of the past for the air force, but there were still thousands of

P-51s available, even though most of them were beginning to show their age. As the 51 was moved out of
the air-superiority role, especially with the delivery of
more F-86s to the front, it became one of the primary
ground strike aircraft for the remainder of the war.

However, as the war progressed, especially after the
stabilization of the front, the missions for the P-51 became increasingly difficult as Colonel Raymond Mc-
Kelvey with the old 18th Fighter Wing discovered.

Colonel Raymond McKelvey
18th Fighter Wing

The people that I remember best and the events I remember best were the ones involving the Korean war-
riors. They stand out; they are leaders; they are very
normal people. But as soon as they strap on their bird,
they become something different. They're not glassy-
eyed killers, they're skilled pilots. They have a job to
do, and they're going to do it to the very best of their
ability. And if they are leading or following, it will be
the best they know how to do. Denis Earp [of the South
African air force] was one of those great men.

We were on a group gaggle, as we called it, and we
got up over the middle of North Korea, and all of a
sudden there were some MiGs that we hadn't expected
to see that far south. Well, the group kind of broke into
them, and as we broke, one of them made a passing
shot through our squadron.

I thought, "Damn it, if I can get a shot at a MiG, I'm
going to take it!" And I let fly with a few .50s. But as I
was coming on around, I saw this streak of rockets go-

ing off. Denis Earp had not only broken into them, he'd fired his *air-to-ground* rockets after them! He was on flak suppression, and he had PT fuses for air burst, and he thought, "Just on the odd chance one of them might reach that sucker . . ." So he broke into them and fired all six rockets.

The MiGs broke off. They broke off and went home. So we reassembled and went on with our mission— those of us that were on that side of the group. As our squadrons broke, of course, we jettisoned bombs very quickly, so all we could do was attack with rockets when we finally got there. But Denis was singlehand- edly effective in breaking off, we don't know how many MiGs. I saw three—somebody claimed there were as many as a dozen up there—but, nonetheless, there were no more attacks. The MiG pilots just de- cided that discretion was the better part of valor!

Rescue Mission

Another mission we were on was when one of my friends, Ken Stewart, was shot down. He was in the river, south of Pyongyang. He'd had his prop shot off, so he wasn't going anywhere. But when we got him back, he said, "Boy, without a prop that bird's a won- derful flyer."

When Ken got over the river, he bailed out. We were trying to get a rescue plane in to him, but the guns on the shore were busy shooting at him. He turned his raft over, and hid under it. It had a blue bottom just like the water to help keep the visibility down. Well, comes late in the afternoon, he's in the water, and we're trying to get him, and all of a sudden it's getting kind of dark. And he just about disappeared. The guns are shooting.

We could see the muzzle flashes from the shore. They're not laying on a heavy fire, but every time they think they see something in the river, they open fire.

Well, the Dumbo [rescue plane] isn't going to be too happy if they can shoot across the river. So we had to do some fire suppression as the Dumbo started in. We put the P-51's gear down, we put the flaps down, and at about 170 mph we strafed. That was Joe Pabasa's idea. Putting flaps down got our nose low enough so that we didn't have to strafe out of a dive; we could be at a much shallower dive. And with the landing lights on the gear, we illuminated the guns, so even when they didn't flash, we got them.

The Dumbo came in. Poor old Ken was out there with two waterproof flashlights—two 59-cent, A-cell battery penlights. Neither of the waterproof flashlights worked, and he'd been in the water all this time. Dumbo, in the meantime, makes one orbit and tells us, "We don't have him in sight. We're going to have to get out of here." Suddenly there was a pinpoint of light, and Ken's little penlight showed up. So the Dumbo goes in, makes one pass, scoops him out of the water, and goes home.

A Memorable Raid

Oh, God, those last few missions were horrors. You've just about got your ticket to the Big PX, but you're afraid somebody else is going to punch it with a Quad 50 [four .50-caliber machine guns mounted to a single frame and capable of sending up a murderous hail of bullets]. And it happened. I know people who went down their last three or four missions. There's a story that involves another warrior named Bill Green. He was killed in Korea. We started some low-level raids on

Pyongyang—I guess in June or July of '51—just before
the truce talks started. Bill Green was leading our
squadron. We were going on a low-level napalm raid. In
fact, the whole Fifth Air Force went in there that day.

We had some rather nasty targets in downtown
Pyongyang. I was flying Bill Green's element—number
three—and I had a wonderful wingman named Red
Backman. Now, General Rogers [Turner C. Rogers
was in command of the 18th Fighter-Bomber Wing]
flew all the nasty missions with us. He did not lead—
he said he wanted his most experienced combat people
in the lead—so he flew Bill Green's wing as number
two, and I was right behind him.

After the briefing, Bill came over, put his arm around
my shoulder, and said, "Mac, let's go over here and talk
for a minute." So we got out of everybody's earshot,
and he huddled up with me and said, "Mac, you know
who's flying my wing. It's General Rogers. I don't care
if your napalms don't hit the ground; your job is to take
care of anything that might shoot General Rogers." So
he told me exactly how to fly the formation. "Lag back
a little bit, get off to the side so that you can keep your
eye on anything that would imperil the general, because if anything happens to him, I don't even want to
think about what's going to happen to you."

Now, on this raid we got some flak, but the real
close-in defenses—the Quad 50s and so forth—were
all built into pits. So we just stayed low enough that
they really couldn't get a bead on us. We saw stuff going over our heads like mad. We'd pretty much gone
into almost a string of flights abreast. The flights were
stacked—one, two, three, four—almost a trail. And I
was watching for anything that might threaten General
Rogers.

I flew past the gun pit, and I could see the slants on their eyes. I could also see the guns traversing, and I thought, "Uh, oh! I'm in for it this time 'cause they're going to come up my tail."

About the time I was thinking that and starting to move over to the side to give them a little harder shot—make them traverse even more—here comes this very quiet voice, the fellow we called "The Quiet Man" in the squadron, my wingman, Red Backman. He calls me, and he says, "Joyce Three, I've got him."

I was up on a wing turning, and I looked back, and there was Red. I don't know how he got up and down so quickly. He got his guns on them and blew that gun pit out of existence. He gave them a dose of .50 calibers. How he did it, I'll never know.

McKelvey survived his tour, as did General Rogers. While he and the general were pounding targets around Pyongyang, President Truman had already made it clear that the campaign would no longer be pursued to a final victory.

This confusing war had changed yet again, and gone were the overly optimistic days of the previous fall when it was felt that the aggressive government of North Korea could be wiped off the map and our troops would be coming home before Christmas. The strategic plan now was to bring it to a swift conclusion at the negotiating table, by agreeing to a return to the status quo prior to June 25, 1950, establishing a border between North and South Korea essentially along the same line it held before, or along the now static front line.

With the decision not to press for a decisive victory

by the allies, and the blunting of the Chinese "Big Red Attacks," of April and May, the front line finally settled into a static front that looked like a throwback to 1916. Trenches, fortress strong points, defenses in depth festooned with oceans of barbed wire, both sides dug in deep. World War I–style battles would rage for days over a minor hilltop, burned-out village or river crossing, the landscape cratered like the moon from incessant bombardments. The only difference was that one side still used World War I tactics of massed bayonet charges that would cost thousands, even tens of thousands of casualties. The United Nations forces increasingly relied on massed artillery and close-in interdiction strikes from above.

The Chinese viewed these battles as yet another chip on the negotiating table, a clear demonstration of their willingness to spend hundreds of thousands of lives if need be to gain their position. It was a clear and pitiless challenge by a totalitarian state, striking at the inherent weakness of a republic. George Marshall had once mused that no democracy can withstand a seven-year war; eventually the people would seek a negotiated way out of the struggle rather than endure the continued losses. Through the bitter and protracted struggle along the front lines, the Chinese strategy now became one of bleeding us into an agreement of their design. The Chinese believed that eventually Congress would feel the pressure from the voters questioning why their sons were being sent to die in an unwinnable war and would force the government to cut its losses, drop its cards, and fold. It was a strategy that would indeed work twenty years later, in Vietnam.

Proponents of the air force can argue with some strength that it was airpower that was the single biggest factor in preventing such a capitulation in Korea. With near complete air superiority over the actual battlefield it was impossible for the Chinese to mass, let alone bring up sufficient supplies for an offensive blow big enough to bloody the United Nations into submission. In fact, after the annihilation rained down from above after the "Big Red Attacks," the Chinese never again mustered enough troops and supplies for another all-out offensive in Korea.

Farther north, the air force repeatedly went after the North Korean airfields, preventing any significant buildup below the Yalu. On this front, though, the cost was higher than over the static battlefield. The B-29s, which roamed at will along the 38th parallel, were proving vulnerable to the slashing attacks of MiGs streaking in from the other side of the Yalu. Assigned the task of pounding the airfields in the northern part of Korea, by the middle of October, B-29s were encountering increasing resistance. In fact, the Chinese were planning a deadly surprise.

Throughout the summer the Chinese were secretly building up their air force, with hundreds of MiGs coming across the border from Russia. No longer fearing a major allied air force strike north of the Yalu, they constructed dozens of new airfields, many of them within sight of the river.

This rapid buildup of MiGs caught the allied command by surprise; in fact, by the end of October the Chinese could actually put more air superiority fighters into the skies than FEAF—more than 400 MiGs against less than 200 Sabres. Given the ground turnaround time and "commuting" distance to the Yalu, Sabre pilots were typically facing odds of four and five to one. With this sudden and dramatic change in numbers, the Chinese became bolder and started to send "Big Wing" fighter sweeps across the Yalu, looking for a fight and especially looking for prop bombers like the B-26 and B-29.

In response, fighter escort size was increased, often to a ratio of three to four fighters for every bomber. On October 22, 1951, nine Superforts from 19th Group went in against enemy positions at Taechon, escorted by twenty-four Thunderjets.

The F-84 Thunderjet was the heaviest fighter-bomber in our arsenal. It proved itself quite capable as a ground support aircraft, and would increasingly take over that role from the P-51, but it was a slow, lumbering giant compared to the agile MiG 15. Given the shortage of Sabres, Thunderjets were usually assigned the escort role for B-26 and B-29 strikes.

During the October 22 strike, the F-84's shortcomings became evident, along with the change in Chinese tactics. Shortly after the 29s bombed the target, a mass formation of forty MiGs charged in. The Thunderjets broke away from tight escort, moving out to contain the attack. Suddenly three MiGs, hiding in the cloud cover, dived into the unescorted Superforts, attacked, and went through the formation of bombers. The attack hit so fast that not a single shot was fired in reply. One of the Forts was hit so badly that it barely made it to the coast. The crew bailed out over the ocean and were picked up. The Chinese had dropped a heavy bomber.

It was an evil portent of what would come the following day.

On the twenty-third, nine Superforts from the 307th Bombardment Wing were scheduled to hit the North Korean airfield at Namsi. Before the mission was even into Korean airspace, the battle was on over MiG Alley. Thirty-four F-86 Sabres were assigned as a blocking force along the Yalu. They were jumped by over one hundred MiGs! Two MiGs went down in flames, but the Sabres were pinned to their own fight.

The 307th had rendezvoused with fifty-five Thunderjets, an escort ratio of nearly seven to one (the strike was down to eight B-29s, with one of the bombers aborting short of the target). Approximately fifty MiGs closed in on the package of bombers and fighters and started to circle, trying to lure the Thunderjets into a fight. In such an encounter, a chase of but ten seconds could put an escort completely out of support range, and the Thunderjets refused the bait.

The lead section of three bombers turned for final approach to their target and the MiGs, dropping their bait tactics, made a head-on charge into the lead formation. The first B-29, piloted by Captain Thomas Shields, was torn apart and caught on fire, but he held the course. All three planes in his section were severely damaged, and as they broke away after their bomb run, there was an apparent lapse in communications with the escorts. The three badly damaged bombers were alone and the MiGs swarmed in from every direction.

In the last war, a fighter that attempted a climbing approach against the belly of a B-29 was asking for trouble, but a jet fighter could now pull such a maneuver and streak up through a formation at 400 mph. MiGs came straight up from below, while others dived in from above.

The second and third formations each lost a bomber as they turned clear of the target after dropping their bombs. Captain Shields heroically stayed at the controls of his dying aircraft, barely making the coast. His surviving crew were able to bail out, but Shields went down with his plane.

The insides of the 29s were an inferno. Explosions racked the crew compartments, instruments were shot away, blood was splattered against canopies, flames ignited, and still the MiGs tore away at the lumbering giants.

The five surviving bombers staggered back, most of the planes so badly shot up they were out of the war. The Thunderjet was completely outclassed in the fight. Three kills were credited to the gunners on board the bombers; only one went to the Thunderjets, an even exchange, since one F-84 went down as well. The after-action report for the 307th Bombardment Wing stated that a minimum of 150 Sabres would have been needed to hold back the enemy attacks.

The following day approximately fifty MiGs tore into another formation of eight B-29s sent to take out a railroad bridge at Sunchon. Again the escorts, this time ten F-84s and sixteen Australian Meteors, proved inadequate. The MiGs chased the B-29s all the way back to the eastern coast, dropping one of the Superforts into Wonsan Harbor.

Several days later, daylight raids by B-29s were suspended. Prior to this bloody week, the air force had lost a total of six B-29s to hostile action since the start of the war. In one week, five B-29s had gone down, eight more were seriously damaged, fifty-five crew members were dead or missing, and twelve had been wounded.

With the suspension of heavy bombardment raids, the Chinese actually moved dozens of fighters to air bases south of the Yalu, in part to act as bait. North of the Yalu mass formations of MiGs, sometimes numbering 200 or more, would gather, darkening the skies, and then climb to 50,000 feet, half a mile above the ceiling of the Sabre.

Crossing the border, the MiGs would maneuver back and forth, obviously practicing battle skills, tantalizingly out of reach of the vastly outnumbered Sabres lingering below. Sometimes days would pass without contact, the MiGs putting on massive air shows above the Sabres. If a lone Sabre pilot foolishly wandered off from his own formation, he would be swarmed. This enraging game of one-way tag would go on for days at a time, and then, without warning, the mass formation of MiGs would pounce, slashing down for a quick exchange, then climbing back up beyond range, or skirting across the border into the safe zone north of the river. It is no wonder that the Sabre pilots forced to endure this one-sided encounter raged over the limits of their aircraft and the limits placed upon them by their leaders.

It wasn't until the fall of 1952 that the air force finally received an upgraded version of the Sabre that could truly match the MiG. This was the legendary F-86F. Engine power was increased by 15 percent, so that finally American pilots had a machine capable of going faster than the MiG in level flight, thus providing the key edge of deciding when and when not to offer battle. Wing, tail, and elevators were modified based upon the hard experiences learned in Korea, providing more maneuverability, especially when approaching Mach 1.

A new radar-guided gunsight was added. After a one-second lockon, the sight adjusted according to range, a crucial technological development for air battles being fought at 600 mph. The one frustrating advantage the MiGs would maintain till the end of the war was service ceiling: they could still climb above the range of the Sabres, then remain out of reach until skirting back over the border into China.

This was the new paradigm for the next two years of air combat. The Chinese had the key advantage of safe havens to operate out of, enabling them to decide when and where battle would be offered. If the battle turned the wrong way, a race upstairs to 50,000 feet gave them safety for the return flight home.

New tactics had to be developed for this new type of war, controlled by the constraints deriving from concern that a limited war in Korea could at any time turn into a global nuclear holocaust. Colonel Frederick "Boots" Blesse, having survived flipping a P-51, was one of the leaders pressing for the design of tactics to counter the advantages now held by the Chinese.

11

EVOLVING TACTICS AND THE NEED FOR TRAINING

Colonel Frederick "Boots" Blesse finished out his first tour and returned to the States, where he devoted his efforts to studying and refining tactics for use in Korea. The navy and the air force had yet to create a "Top Gun"–type program, so many pilots relied upon on-the-job training, usually shepherded along by an experienced pilot like Boots, who came back into the fight early in 1952, this time flying an F-86. Upon his return, Blesse set out on a crusade to upgrade the combat skills of his pilots and to press the attack home on the MiGs.

General Frederick "Boots" Blesse

Learning the New Tactics

They had tactics in World War II and, in some cases, the commander himself wrote down some things that were tactics, but basically we didn't have a whole lot of information. I didn't know how the unit was going to operate. That was left more to the wing commander. When I got there, they had been flying sixteen ship missions or even twenty or twenty-four ship missions. It really wasn't a smart way to do things, because everybody left practically at the same time. So by the time you came back, everybody was low on fuel at the same time. That wasn't a very smart maneuver, so we began sending the flights off about five minutes apart, four aircraft at a time.

That worked out a lot better, because it extended our coverage of the area. You had F-86s up there for two hours at a time instead of an hour and twenty minutes.

Now, the other thing was, how were you going to fight? That's the thing that wasn't really passed on from World War II. When I first got there, everybody that went into a squadron—it didn't matter whether you were a colonel, major, lieutenant, or captain—you were going to fight at least ten or fifteen missions on a wing. Then you'd fly another ten or fifteen missions as an element leader before anyone would trust you to lead in a fight.

During those twenty or thirty missions you picked up a lot about how things were, what they expected you to do, etc., and you started looking for what could be improved. I went through that period and was very unhappy with the setup. They had the wingmen spread out so far on your wing—way out to the right—so far away, it was difficult to tell if he was a MiG or an F-86!

One of my main points was that you're up there offensively, *not* defensively. If you're up there offensively, you have to expect that you're going to maneuver. And, if you're going to maneuver, the first thing that's going to happen to that guy half a mile out there on your wing is that you're going to lose him. If you turn into him, he'll never make the turn in a million years.

Now, when I was going through this, I was a maintenance officer for about thirty days. Then the squadron commander rotated, they fired the Operations officer, and I came in as the new Operations officer. One of the first things I wanted to do—there were some guys in the outfit leading flights who weren't capable of leading. They didn't want to find MiGs, and when they did, they didn't know what to do with them.

I wanted to sort that out and get those guys transferred out. I wanted people in there who really wanted to fight the war. We did that. I fired two flight commanders and brought in two younger guys who were a lot better airplane drivers and knew more about what they were doing.

The major thing, though, was that I sat down and wrote procedures about the way we were going to do things. I showed where the leader should be; here is where the number two man is going to fly, and you've got to be close enough that you can read the numbers on his tail. If you can't read the numbers on his tail, he is probably going to get lost if you do a maximum performance turn into him. And he can't be line abreast with you; he's got to be back along about a 45-degree angle. That way he can slide underneath you a little bit, slide to the outside, then pull back, and you can expect to have a wingman.

The idea that the wingman has got to be looking to the rear all the time is fallacious. If he's looking to the rear at the time the leader makes a sharp turn, you're never going to see him again. So, when the fight first starts, from then on the wingman tries to look to the rear whenever he has an opportunity and gives a call to the leader that he's clear. That's the best you can do.

During the maneuvering phase, which is usually rather violent, the leader may make a hard turn, perhaps dive down, then pull out of a four- to six-G turn and reverse and pull around—well, the wingman is never going to be looking around at that time. And we don't want him looking around at that time! Everybody seemed to realize this, but nobody would put it on paper and say, "This is the way we're going to operate." That's what I did.

So we put it in concrete that the number two and the number four men always stayed with number one and number three. If the elements got separated, three and four were a fighting team and one and two were a fighting team. We'll fight as a four-ship flight as long as we can. If there's two targets, then the lead element would take one of them and the number three and four man element would take the other.

Those were some basic changes we made, and we were making those changes in the latter part of April and May of '52. I think I got my first kill in late May, then another kill in early June, but the MiGs were really not flying very much then. So I told the guys, "Look, this is kind of like professional golf. A professional golfer would never think of going two weeks or even a week without hitting a lot of practice balls and getting ready to play in the tournament. Now, he's only playing for money; we're playing for our lives here. The way we've been doing this thing, you guys may go thirty to thirty-five missions and never see an enemy airplane. When all of a sudden you do, you're out of practice. The things that you do are not as sharp as they would be if you'd been practicing. So here's a new rule: every time you go on a mission, if you don't see MiGs, you come back about five minutes early. Then the leader and the number two man as an element will have a fight with the number three and four men. They'll do a few turns, and one element will try to get on the other until you get down to minimum fuel, and then you come in and land. And not only that, but I want every flight commander to have a chart in his boardroom so that I can walk in and see every time the number three man or the number four man gets in a fight. I don't care if it's with a MiG or another F-86. I want to see an 'X' by his name. If he goes more than a week without an 'X' by his name, you're going to have to take him on a training mission. I don't think you want to waste your time doing that."

It was early in August of '52 that the MiGs started suddenly to fly for some reason. We went up around the beginning of August, and we'd had two months of practicing the new tactics. We finally got into a big donnybrook with the MiGs that day. One outfit didn't get any kills, as I recall, and another got one, and we got about four. Not only that, but all four wingmen stayed with their leaders. In the other outfit that got a kill, that leader got it by himself. The wingman was lost, and the leader got the kill and came back by himself. You could very easily have lost a guy's life doing that.

Before we started all this new training, we had times where we went sixty days without getting a kill in our outfit. The other squadron—the 335th—was doing a little better. They were getting maybe three or four. The 336th wasn't doing any better than we were. But starting in August we got about twenty-two or twenty-three kills. In September we had a little bit more than that, just in our outfit. There was a dramatic increase in proficiency. There were guys who thought we were barking up the wrong tree when we changed all the tactics.

It was August before we had a full squadron of people who really believed in what the hell we were doing. It really wasn't done in a dictatorial fashion, but what we were doing [before] wasn't working. There were reasons it didn't work, so I just showed that what we were going to do from now on was going to work and why. You've got to practice and know what you're doing.

I took each one of the four flight commanders out, and I flew with each of them. I didn't tell them we were going to change anything. I just told them, "We're going to fly. You fly my wing, and we'll do some maneuvering and see how things go." I didn't give him a briefing or anything. So he got out there in a good position, and I started about a four G turn into him.

Of course, he couldn't make the turn and stalled and dropped a thousand feet or so. I whipped over the back and just slid right in behind him. I called him and said, "Have you got me in sight?" He said, "No, I haven't got you." I called back and said, "Okay, I'm turning to the right, and I'm directly behind you." So we went up and did this again, and this time he wasn't quite as far forward, but he still hadn't gotten the message completely.

About the fourth time, he's in there about a 45-degree angle behind me, and I can read the numbers on his tail. When I took him into a four G turn that time, he stayed with me all the way around. I reversed the turn, went up over the top, and down through Immelmans [a half loop in which the plane levels out at the top of the loop]—we did everything known to man—and when we finished, the guy's right there on my wing.

We came back in and I asked him, "Joe, at first you had a real nice position way out there line abreast with me, then at the end you were flying so close. Why did you change your position?" And he said, "Jeeze! The way you were racking that airplane around, you can't expect me to be able to fly on your wing out there like that! The turns are too tight, and I was too far away." I said, "Okay, you just learned chapter one. This is exactly what I want you to teach the guys in your flight." And I think they got about four or five training missions per day in each flight.

I had gotten permission from the wing commander, Colonel "Bud" Mahurin, to get off the combat schedule for about a week. He was reluctant to do that, but he said okay. Unfortunately, Bud got shot down in early May, so he never saw our squadron come to life. He just found it out by looking at the statistics after the war was over.

Flying Against MiGs (Tactics)

The MiGs usually flew one mission per day, while we flew three missions to make sure we didn't miss them. After eighty-eight missions, I had two kills on my side. After that, I either got lucky or the MiGs started flying. I got a couple more before my ninety-fourth mission and at that time, you had to declare whether you were going to extend or whether you were going to go home.

If you wanted to extend for another twenty-five missions, you had to state that so they wouldn't put in for a replacement for you. You had to tell them that by your ninety-fifth mission. I did that. I wanted to get that last MiG if I could.

I got my fifth kill about the fourth of September in '52. A few days later I got two, then I got another.

The fact that you didn't see the MiGs every time you went up really led in some cases to bad tactics. If you hadn't seen a MiG for thirty-five missions and suddenly you've got one, well, it's not as easy to let that guy go as it would be if you saw MiGs every time you were up there. You wanted to get something out of your mission, so a lot of times you did things that weren't sound tactically. You really pushed it.

Pushing it is exactly what Colonel Blesse did, with near-fatal consequences.

A Harrowing Flight and an Air-Sea Rescue

I never really doubted that I was going to get home. But on my 121st mission, I had a guy with me who was not very experienced. We used to take the people who had less than ten missions. We made it a habit to put those with flight commanders who had kills, who had gotten into combat and had gotten a victory or two. Because if you check the new guys out with the guys that fly as though they really want to do something, the new ones end up being a lot better themselves.

If you send them up there with Casper Milquetoast and then on the fifteenth mission they go with one of these guys that really wants to fly it, they come back thinking, "Jeeze, this guy's crazy! He's gonna kill us all." We'd always make sure they had two or three missions with those, and I had one of those guys this time—he was on his second mission.

We milled around up there, but there wasn't a lot of activity, so we finally decided we'd start home. We were pretty far north—well north of Sinuiju—when we started back. On the way back, the guys who were controlling the radar said we had a flight at six o'clock at about 15 miles, so we couldn't see anything. By then they were letting down, and we did see them. They continued to close on us.

Now, there were only two of us at this point. The number four man had a tank that didn't feed, and number three went home with him, so there was just this other guy and myself. I thought, "Well, instead of cruising along here this way, we'll start letting down, and that'll make it more difficult for the MiGs to close on us."

But they had a head of speed, I guess, and they got down to where we could see them very quickly. I kept an eye on them, and I knew they were way out of firing range, but the leader had a 37-millimeter gun. Unfortunately, the 37-millimeter had a very peculiar characteristic, in that when he fired at you, you could see that round coming. It was like a Roman candle that you see on the Fourth of July. You could see it coming, and after it went by you could still see it going away from you as well. With tracers, you can't see that at all, but if you look in front of you, you'll see what looks like little dots of white going all over the place, because he's missing you.

These other things scared the new guy. The MiG was firing out of range. I could see that the 37-millimeter cannon was falling several thousand feet behind my guy, so there really wasn't a big problem. Very shortly we were going to be crossing out over the water. MiGs don't want to chase you over the water.

So I figured we were in pretty good shape. But my wingman was behind me farther than I wanted him to be, and I called him at least three times and told him to close it. He was slow in doing that and, of course, it got more difficult for him to do it when I decided we needed to pick up the speed a little bit.

For one reason or another while the lead MiG was firing that 37-millimeter cannon way out of range, my wingman thought he was going to get hit and made a sharp turn to the left—broke away from me. He called and said, "I'm breaking left. This guy's gonna hit me." I called him back and said, "Hold your course. Hold your course; she's way out of range," but he had already done it.

Well, I couldn't just let him go, so I whipped around to the left and, of course, that's exactly what the lead MiG was trying to get him to do. The minute he turned to the left, the MiG cut him off severely to the left and closed in to what turned out to be reasonable firing range. We were at about 19,000 or 20,000 feet by that time, so I called my number two man and told him, "Keep that thing at a four G turn, keep the nose low, and I'm coming in behind you." We did that, getting down to about 15,000 or 16,000 feet.

The lead MiG was between myself and my wingman, but I got in behind the wingman of the leader, who was not quite as good a pilot, and I fired at him. When I hit him he broke off, and then he must have called the leader, since the leader broke off, too.

I called my number two man and said, "Okay. Straighten it out. Take up this heading and climb to thirty-five thousand feet and go. I'll be all right."

So he took off and got back okay. In the meantime, when I eased up to fire at the number two MiG, the number three and number four men dropped behind me. There were four MiGs and only two of us. So now the three and the four men were in the shooting position behind me. I continued on descending myself and keeping a lot of Gs on it. I finally threw those two MiGs to the outside of the turn, reversed the turn, went over the top, and the MiGs took a 180-degree turn and got out of there. That was exactly what I wanted. I didn't want to fight with them—I didn't have enough fuel to do that.

I made about a 120-degree turn to get back on course for home. By this time I was at about 8,000 feet. I started climbing up, and about fifteen seconds later, out of the corner of my eye, on the left, letting down about 4,000 or 5,000 feet above me, is a single MiG.

I thought, "Oh, my God, school's out. If I have to turn with this guy, I'm going to end up a POW up here." Well, the guy never saw me. He continued to let down—flew right across in front of me and never saw me—and I thought, "Well, it's kind of a toss-up as to whether I get home or not." The next thought that crossed my mind was, "Why not?"

I pulled to the right to cut him off and close the range, slid in behind him, shot him down, reversed course again, and headed out toward home, but it still took me more fuel than I had. I don't think I'd have made it even if I hadn't engaged the MiG, because I couldn't have wasted a hundred pounds of fuel on that guy. All I did was make a 90-degree turn and shoot him, then turn back 90 degrees again.

We had certain procedures that had been developed in our squadron that if you got over Pyongyang at 35,000 feet, you could shut the engine down and glide and still hit the traffic pattern at Tienpo at about 5,000 feet. That was enough to get a start and make one big wide circle to be sure you had power to land it.

So that was my objective, and I started climbing up and climbing up and climbing up, and I got up to about—Jeeze, I can't remember exactly what—but it wasn't anywhere near 35,000 feet. Seemed to me I got up to around 23,000 or something like that, and I decided that unless I had a really good tailwind, I wasn't going to make this.

Now, there was a group of guys that always sat in the Ready Room and listened to all the combat channels to hear the fights or whatever was going on, and you had a weather guy that was always in there, too. So I called in on that channel and asked to talk to Storm [the weather officer].

I asked him, "What are the winds right now at thirty thousand at twenty-five and twenty?" He gave me winds that were not tailwinds. They were crosswinds, and I was getting about 10 degrees of headwinds. Well, that wasn't going to help me any, so I said, "Well, I'm going to head for the island of Pen Yang Do. There's about four or five thousand feet of beach there. I'll put the 86 down on Pen Yang Do if I can get there."

Then I went over to the Air-Sea Rescue channel and called an Air-Sea Rescue boat that always stood in the area and told them, "Don't go home yet. Come down the coastline—south along the coast—until you get opposite Pen Yang Do, then circle. I'll be there very shortly."

He was practically in that area already. By this time I was down to about 17,000 feet, and I turned to the west to go toward Pen Yang Do. I was getting fired at by a lot of flak, but I didn't have enough airspeed to be turning left and right and evading it, so I just held it on course and hoped those guys couldn't hit me.

I shut the engine down when I got down to about 400 pounds. I was gliding to the west, letting down from 17 to 15 to 13, etc., when I crossed a main supply route. Those were always very, very well guarded with flak and stuff of that nature. Boy, I picked up a tremendous amount of rounds of fire from that, and right around 7,000 feet, I decided I was going to get hit if I didn't do something.

So I started the engine up and climbed back up a ways and I got up to about 9,000 or 10,000 feet. Then the airplane engine just quit; out of fuel. So I lowered the nose and stuck it down to 180 knots, which was for best gliding speed. I was still over the land at this time, and I was getting a little concerned whether I was going to make the coast or not. I kept going and finally crossed the coastline at about maybe 2,500 to 3,000 feet and continued out over the ocean. I was in constant contact by this time with the Air-Sea Rescue, and I told him what heading I was on, where I was, and what altitude.

He said, "Roger, I have you in sight," and I said, "Okay, don't get too close, because when I bail out of this thing I don't know where the airplane is going to go, and you're going to have to avoid this F-86." "That's okay," he said, "you go ahead."

When I got between 3,000 feet and 2,000 feet, I'm gliding down and I had just talked to the weather guy, and I told him, I said, "Okay, Stormy. That's it. I can't make Pen Yang Do and I'm going to have to bail out. I've got an Air-Sea Rescue guy here and I'm going to punch out here in about another thirty seconds."

A pilot sits in the cockpit of an F-51 named "Oh-Kay Baby" at K-14.
(Photograph by Stan Newman)

Two Corsairs that collided at Kimpo in September of 1950.
(Photograph by Ray Stewart)

Two crew members prepare a B-26 Invader for a mission (263rd Fighter-Bomber Wing). A sign hanging from one of the nose guns reads HOT GUNS. *(Photograph by Al Keeler)*

Three RF-80s parked in the snow. *(Photograph by Jim Hanson)*

A dragonfly helicopter on board the USS *Saipan*. *(Photograph by George Chesterfield)*

Major Sharp bellies in with armed rockets in April of 1951. *(Photograph by Jack Coor)*

Thirty-seven-millimeter MiG damage to the engine of an F-80 in May of 1951. *(Photograph by Jack Coor)*

Two F-86s in tight formation. *(Photograph by John Africa)*

Six F-94s of the 319th FIS fly over Seoul. *(Photograph by Sam Lyons)*

A crane hoists an F-84E of the 27th FEW up onto the deck of the USS *Bataan* in November of 1950. *(Photograph by D. Watt)*

Stepping down from the cockpit, Captain Ralph Parr receives word that the truce has been signed. *(Courtesy of Ralph Parr)*

K-14: An RF-80 that appears to be a photo recce aircraft, since the upper surfaces have been sprayed with OD green (camouflage). *(Photograph by Stan Newman)*

Rear view of an F-80 tail with flak damage to the port elevator. *(Photograph by Jack Coor)*

An F-94 in flight over Suwon (319th FIS). *(Photograph by Ed Cooke)*

Two flights of F-86s in close formation. *(Photograph by K. Dittmer)*

Two F-84s, piloted by Captain Reynolds and H. Brennan, head down for Suwon. *(Photograph by Spry)*

Armament crews load 500-pound GP bomb and five-inch rockets. Note the fancy bomb hoist gear being used. *(Photograph by Duane Biteman)*

Two F-86s climb skyward just after take-off in April of 1952. *(Photograph by M. Bambrick)*

Thirty-seven-millimeter MiG damage to an F-84 at Kay2. May, 1951.
(Photograph by Jack Coor)

An F-84 of the 159th Fighter Squadron flies over Japan in 1950.
(Photograph by H.W. Rued)

By that time a lot of guys had heard that I was in trouble and were collecting in the Ops Room where the radio was. One guy grabbed the radio and said, "You redheaded so-and-so, you get back here. You owe me ten bucks!" And another grabbed it and said, "Good luck, buddy; we'll see you at supper." Maybe four or five guys just grabbed the mike and said one little thing.

I'll tell you, it sent chills up and down my spine. I was about to pull the handles here, and the only thought in my mind was, "God, what a marvelous bunch of guys." At that, I undid my safety belt and got rid of the harness and all that, so that the minute the seat and I got into the slipstream, the seat would be blown away from me. (I had read in some kind of a safety report or something that this was a good thing to do.) Well, I did that, and that worked just fine.

The parachute opened; everything was fine. I got down into the water and swam around there, got my dinghy open, and my Mae West inflated and that sort of thing. I climbed into the dinghy, then realized that the pockets of my flight suit had been opened at the bottom, and my maps and a bunch of other stuff like that were floating around the water.

I paddled the dinghy over and picked up my maps, and by this time the SA 2 had landed pretty close to me. He had taxied up to within twenty-five yards of where I was, and the back end of the SA 2 was open and a guy was there—he had what looked like a flare gun to me—and he shot a line way out over the top of my dinghy.

I grabbed the line, pulled myself over to the side of the airplane, then held on to the rope while those guys pulled me up into the back end of the SA 2. My dinghy was still down there, along with the rest of whatever else I had, and the minute I got in the back, this guy guns it and starts taxiing away.

I ran up to the front and said, "Hey, wait a minute! Wait a minute! I haven't got my stuff out of my dinghy yet." And he said, "The hell with your dinghy! We're getting the hell out of here." I found out later that was the first time he had picked anybody up within rifle range of the enemy. He flew me back to the base at Tienpo, and we had a big party that night. The next day I went over to Seventh Air Force and met with a bunch of generals and reporters, and found out I was a leading ace—I had ten at that time.

Returning stateside in October 1952, Colonel Blesse pushed for intensified training prior to committing new pilots to operations in Korea.

Teaching Tactics Stateside

When I came back after my 121st mission in October of 1952, they sent me to Nellis Air Force Base. I had the 3,596th F-86 training squadron. Out of that squadron there was a tremendous amount of experience. I think at one time we had around twenty-five jet aces. In my squadron we started teaching the same sort of stuff that I had taught over in Korea, because the guys who came through Nellis were all going over to Korea.

The other training squadrons were teaching something different. The group commander, Colonel Bruce Hinton, called me in and said he understood we were teaching different tactics. He wanted to know why, so I explained to him where I got it and why we did it over in Korea. He thought it was great and went to the other four squadrons and dictated that all of them would use the same tactics.

Then we formed a tactics team in my outfit. The navy and the marines heard about it, and we started getting requests for us to fly with them. They'd come in on the weekend, and we'd fly two or three missions with them, then write up a little report to tell them what they had to do to improve their tactics.

Lessons Learned in Korea (Nearly Lost in Vietnam)

In the fifteen years between the end of Korea and 1968, there was a big change. By that time we had IR [infrared] missiles, radar missiles, and we initially had no gun. They had taken the guns off the airplanes. Because during that period back in the States, our "tacticians"—I use the word loosely—had determined that there was no need for the gun now that we had the missile. It was screwy.

Another jet ace and I went to the Pentagon and talked to the brass there. We told them this was a mistake and that we really needed to have the guns on the airplane. And they said, "Oh, you aces are all the same. You shoot down an airplane with a gun, and now you think that's the only way airplanes are going to be shot down. You're going to have to bring yourself up into the modern world. Guns are passé." I said, "This is the last thing I'll say, and I'm not going to say anything else. This reminds me of two guys in a phone booth. One guy has a short blade knife, and the other guy's got a rifle. Now, the rifle is obviously a better piece of equipment, but not in a phone booth. What is the guy going to do when he fires the missile, the missile misses, and the two airplanes are still closing? He ends up in a turning fight with an enemy airplane. What is he going to do with a missile that doesn't even arm itself for a thousand feet? It seems to me that the gun is a necessary thing on the airplane as long as we're going to fight other airplanes."

Well, they didn't agree with that. When I went to Vietnam, I went in as the director of Operations of the 366th Tactical Fighter Wing. The first thing I did was form a tactics section and got them working on putting a gun underneath the F-4. There was already a Su-16 that had a Gatling gun arrangement on it, but nobody was using it. We had Supply get us some, and we put one or two of them on different airplanes. We fought with them, though we didn't tell anybody what we were doing. I'd take a single lead airplane, then put the number two man with the gun. It took a lot of extra fuel, but that didn't matter. We weren't going to operate that way; we were just trying to find out what the difference would be between the leader and the number two man if the number two man had a gun.

We really wanted the leader to have the gun. The number two man was always using a little more fuel than the leader anyway, so the presence of the gun under the lead airplane didn't have even a minor effect as far as fuel was concerned. We experimented doing some fighting and strafing with the gun. We tried putting one on each wing and strafing with those, then we put one on each wing and one on the centerline for short-range missions, since they took the place of the extra fuel tanks. Those guns were invaluable for missions where you'd be going out only 100 or 75 miles and attacking a bunch of ships or skiffs that were coming in across the beach to deliver supplies and such.

After I was convinced that guns were a good idea and not a bad one, I had to go down and get permission to use them. I had to see the same guys that told us we were nuts about four or five years before! They told me then that they thought I had a hole in my head, but they thought it might be a better idea than they'd initially thought. So they said, "Go ahead with it, and keep us informed."

We did that, and I guess it was a week or so later that we had a couple flights up in the area with the guns, and we got a couple of kills with them. Before the war was over, we got a total of seventeen MiGs with the guns, and we did an awful lot of good air-to-ground work. We established the fact that the gun really was a necessity. It was something not only that we *could* use, but that we *had* to use. The next F-4 that came out—the F-4E—had an internal gun, which was the confirmation of our ideas.

12

1952: STILL A HARD FIGHT

Even into the summer and fall of 1952 it was still a hard fight along MiG Alley, in spite of the efforts of men like Colonel Blesse to drive home the lessons hard-won through bitter experience.

Desperate for pilots, the air force continued to call up veterans from the postwar years and men who had fought in the skies over Europe and Japan. Colonel Cecil Foster was one of them. Surviving the transition to this new age of warfare, he went on to a blazing career over MiG Alley, joining the chosen few as a Hot Shot with five kills. On one of his first flights "up north," the still-novice Colonel Foster made his first kill in what stands as most likely the longest-running air-to-air jet encounter in the history of warfare. Though Colonel Foster claimed that training was still minimal for the "real thing," it is apparent that someone had prepared him properly, for throughout this marathon encounter he was dealing with odds of at least ten to one.

Colonel Cecil Foster (ace)
51st Fighter-Interceptor Wing, 51st Fighter-Interceptor Group

Training

When I went to Korea, I felt that I was not really trained well enough. I had just been recalled from civilian status, and I went through a jet refresher. I went right into F-86s—well, I went into F-80s first, and then they picked a certain number of us and upgraded us to F-86s before we went over to Korea. But I didn't really feel I had enough training.

There weren't too many people well qualified in jets at the beginning of the Korean War. I had gone through ten hours of jet training in pilot school in January of 1948. Then I had to take an assignment out of jets for about a year and a half, and then I went to Alaska and got into jets again. I was only in the jets there for about four months. I flew formation and that sort of stuff, but the combat tactics were quite inaccurate as far as I was concerned. When we got over to Korea, we learned by trial and error.

The formations that we flew were a little bit new to everybody. The wing I got into had been flying P-51s up till about six months before I got there. So there was no big amount of experience to be pulled on in the jet. I think we were all in more or less of a learning process as we went through the war. I don't think there was an awful lot of expertise in the air force at the beginning of the Korean War; we gained it through experience there.

First Encounter with MiGs

It was during my first couple or three missions when I actually got involved with the MiGs. The first one was on September 7, 1952. I was on my day off, so I just put my uniform on and took my camera down to the flight line. There was a max effort being flown by the wing that day, and I wanted to take pictures from the flight line. But I could hardly see whoever had what we called the "dirty noses"—with the carbon from the .50-calibers.

When you shot the guns, it "blacked their nose," so you'd look for a guy coming in with a dirty nose. When you saw that, you knew he had some action that day, and everybody would gravitate down toward whichever squadron got the action so you could hear the stories. Everybody was definitely interested in hearing what had happened and how it went on.

So I was down at the flight line, and I was there early enough that none of the wings had come back. I had my camera with me and walked into Operations, and there were some guys sitting around in there. One of the flight leaders or flight commanders was briefing some new troops getting ready to go out on a mission. All the airplanes were pretty well gone. We had some airplanes still in our squadron, because we were the alert squadron for the day. The other two squadrons were to send everything they had; we had some left over. We had four out on alert, and they had been scrambled.

When I walked in, my CT leader—our Ops officer—was there, and we started talking. Headquarters asked, "How many airplanes do you have in commission?" He said, "We've got four that are ready to go." They said, "Well, can you put them up on alert?" He said, "Just a minute; I'll see." So they asked the leader who was the alert flyer that day. "Can you man an alert flight?" He said, "We've got myself and two wingmen, but I don't have an element leader."

Hearing all of this, I said, "I'm one."

The Ops officer said, "It's your day off, Foster. I'll get somebody that's scheduled to fly." Well, he looked, and there wasn't anybody around who was qualified yet—certified to fly element lead. So he said, "I'll let you go out there, and you set up an alert, but as soon as somebody that's scheduled to fly today comes in, I'll have you replaced." I said, "Okay."

I had just started toward the personnel equipment building when the phone rang again—it was a scramble. Lieutenant Samms and his two wingmen were in flying suits ready to go, so they grabbed their helmets first and headed for their airplanes. I had to go change my clothes and get into flying gear to go. After I gathered my gear, I ran out to my airplane.

In the meantime some of the new pilots around the squadron came out with me, and they told me what airplane I had, and they were very helpful. Two guys ran around the airplane, one on each side, to preflight it. The crew chief had plugged in the APU [Auxiliary Power Unit, used to power the plane up and kick the jet engines over], and one of the captains who was brand-new in the squadron but who had more jet time than most people followed me up to the cockpit, jumped up on the nose, straddled it, and reached inside and started my engine while I was strapping in.

By the time I was strapped in, the airplane was all preflighted, the engine was running, and the guy jumped off the nose. They took the chocks out, and away I went. I was the second guy airborne. It was amazing to me that I could get off so fast.

As I got airborne, the flight leader who was just in front of me couldn't get his gear up. They had a procedure we used to drop the gear doors. When maintenance went to work on the airplane on the ground, you pulled the emergency gear handle, the doors would drop open, and they would get in there and do their work. When they got through, they needed to reset the plunger so that the gear would retrack normally on takeoff. Well, they forgot to do that, and during the rapid rush out there, it wasn't checked. So, when he got airborne, he couldn't get his gear up and had to abort.

So I'm airborne on my day off, leading a flight of three people I've never met, never seen, never been briefed with. I didn't have any idea what their names were or anything at the time. I joined up, and we crossed the bomb line, tested our guns, and everything was working fine.

Our policy was you could only go in elements of two into combat. If you were a single airplane, you went home; you didn't stay in combat at all. If you got into combat and were separated, your orders were to get out of there as soon as you could and immediately head for home—not to stay in combat as a single aircraft.

So I sent the third airplane over to Choto Island, and I said, "You go into orbit until we get up there, and once we get to the Yalu River area if we don't need you, why you can go home and land." Well, we continued on up and, sure enough, we got up there with both airplanes working fine, so I sent him on home. I could see in front of us that there were lots and lots of contrails. Since they had a max effort, there was a tremendous amount of airplanes that had been up there, and the GCI [ground controlled interception] told me the reason I was going up was to cover the withdrawal of our airplanes that were getting low on fuel.

So, as we came up there, I saw a lot of contrails and, just before we got to the river, I spotted eight MiGs in elements of two. So I started cutting them off and got on the inside of them, and they started making a turn. We were able to really cut them off then and get right in there behind them. As I was approaching in on them, I got a good position on the tail-end Charlie guy, and my wingman said, "Hey, we got eight more MiGs coming in from about six-thirty." And I said, "Okay, try to keep them in sight."

I got in close enough to take a shot at the tail-end Charlie—the first MiG I shot at. I got one shot at him, and my wingman said, "Break left!" So we broke left and level. The flight that was coming in on us was faster than we were. We were at about 39,000 feet, and you can't really punch it in around a corner up there; you've got to feather-fly it around—you have to be real easy on the controls at that altitude.

So they went sliding on past us to the outside. As they did, I reversed and climbed on up and did a big, loose barrel roll, which lost airspeed and let me drop back in around behind the latter part of their string of eight aircraft. I pulled in behind their number seven man and lined up on him. My wingman cleared me, and I took one shot at the number seven man.

My wingman called out, "Tiger lead, eight more MiGs coming in at seven o'clock."

We didn't spot them soon enough, so we had to

break real hard left and, again, they had the altitude
and they had converted the airspeed coming in on us.
They were going much faster than we were, and we did
the break on in, which killed off more airspeed. They
slid by on the outside again. So I pulled the same maneuver. I pulled my nose up, did a big, loose barrel roll,
and came down behind them.

And this sort of procedure was a cat-and-mouse
game that we played for almost forty-five minutes.
Whenever I let off on the nose of the turnaway to cut
these people off so I could put my gunsight on an airplane, they would begin to turn on the inside.

My wingman, Les Erickson, would get on the inside
of me, because he could continue pulling max turn.
When I would shoot, I'd be falling off the outside,
'cause when you pull the trigger to shoot, the recoil
from the six .50-calibers would slow your airplane
down.

Les was on the inside, so I'd clear him and let him
shoot while I was able to slide down, put my nose out,
pick up some airspeed, and get back on the inside of
the turn again, where I could slide back into position.

Then another airplane was called out. Erickson saw
him first and said, "There's another MiG on your right
side." I got him—I just did a regular old barrel roll and
came down behind the guy, and it looked like he was
trying to join up with us in formation. I don't have any
idea why he was doing this. He didn't try to get behind
us; he pulled in on the side like he was joining in formation. Whether he thought we were MiGs, or whether
he was going to stand there and direct the other people
in on us, I have no idea, but it didn't work for him.

I just rolled out behind him, and he didn't do hardly

anything. He was in a slow left turn, and I went ahead and fired a long burst right in, got lots of hits, then rolled out, and went straight ahead and descended a little bit. I just took several more shots at the guy until Les said, "Wing left!" We broke, and he said, "Eight more MiGs on our tail." It was actually one of the first flights. So we went ahead and broke left, and I noticed that we were just about at our "Bingo" fuel, which meant that we had to head for home. I was about out of ammunition and so was Les. So I said, "Okay. Follow me." We did a modified split "S" and headed for home. We had caught these guys loaded with fuel—real heavy with fuel—and we were almost full of fuel when we got there, so we were operating on the feather edge of our max capability the whole time at that altitude.

When we got home, the only thing we could confirm for each other was one MiG damaged, so that's what we came home and claimed. Because when I was shooting, my wingman was looking behind for the other airplanes, and when he was shooting, I was doing the same thing on his position. But that was on the seventh of September, and the War Claims Board met on the twenty-fifth of September. I didn't even know they had such a thing. I was never expecting anything different, but they called Erickson in and debriefed him again, and I had no idea the reason for this. They didn't explain it to us little junior officers.

But the next day I had a mission in which I came back with two MiGs, and I was informed that made me "three kills," because the night before they upgraded my "damage" to a "kill." So that day I went from zero to three. That was the first combat in which I scored anything. As far as I know, it was the longest, continuous jet combat air-to-air in the Korean War. We were almost forty-five minutes with just two of us, and those little MiGs really weren't scared. We weren't scared either; we were too dumb.

Becoming an Ace

On November 22, 1952, they made me the mission leader for this mission, and I was still a first lieutenant with very limited experience and I didn't know what to do. I had no idea what a mission leader was supposed to do. It was the blind leading the blind. I figured out we were going to escort a Marine total reconnaissance aircraft up as he was to go across the Sui-ho Dam Reservoir. I think the dam had been struck previously, and this mission was to see what the damage was.

So I briefed the mission, and we took off. We went up toward the dam area. As soon as our tanks were dry, we were to drop our tanks and pick up this marine plane (he was slower than we were). So we had to scissors back and forth behind him to stay in position to protect him. My element and I were to stay on the wing—two on each wing of this guy—so the MiGs couldn't come in from underneath or from the front or anything. We figured that this must have been a pretty important mission to send four flights of F-86s to escort just one photo recce airplane.

Well, as we dropped tanks, my tanks would not release. According to the rules, if you couldn't get rid of your tanks, you had to get out of the area. So I took my wingman and turned the mission over to my element lead, and my wingman pulled off as I went off to one side. I couldn't shake the tanks loose, so I started to leave.

I did everything I could think of—pushing the buttons and pushing in on the circuit breaker—but nothing seemed to work. Finally I pulled out the circuit breaker and I left it out for ten or fifteen seconds, pushed it back in again, hit the button again, and the tanks dropped. So I turned around and my flight headed back. I called the guy who was running the mission at that time and said, "I'm trying to come back." He said, "Oh, don't try to. You can't get over too far in front." I thought, "Well, I'll head that direction just in case I can catch 'em. When they turn to head home, I can at least join in and help cover them on the way out."

As I headed back to where I thought they would be, I spotted a flight of six MiGs. So my wingman and I got into a tangle with six MiGs. They came in about 11:30—head-on almost—and we started maneuvering, trying to get on the other's tail. Now, these MiG pilots were really experienced. You could tell you didn't have any beginners in this whole flight. We had our hands full.

We were using every maneuver we could think of— ones that weren't even written in the books. We went from high altitude down to medium altitude back up and down as far as altitude goes, and we tried everything under the sun to get behind each other. It finally got to the point where we were getting low on fuel. We weren't yet below minimums, but it was getting close. So I told my wingman, "On this next pass, let's just keep on going. We'll head on out."

So we made another maneuver similar to a scissors coming across each other. We just dove our noses down and headed for K-13 [Foster's base]. Well, these MiGs continued their turn right around and pulled out behind us—I'd say about 4,000 feet behind us. We were spread out and flying at maximum airspeed; we couldn't go any faster. But we kept going. The MiGs just kept gradually getting closer and closer and closer, and pretty soon they got to the point where I called my wingman, Ed Hepner, and said, "Break left!"

I broke right, so I was on his left side and he was on my right side. If he broke left, I could break right and could try to get the MiG on his tail. Well, just as he broke left, the MiG shot. The bullets hit Ed's canopy and went into the instrument panel. A piece of shrapnel went through his helmet, hitting him in the head. At the same time I told him to break left, he called he was breaking left, and at the same time all that happened, he got hit. I didn't hear him; he didn't hear me.

I was able to get behind the MiG by rolling back around and coming up behind, and I took a long shot at him. His airplane just seemed like it stopped in the air. I pulled the power back to idle and put my speed brakes out, but I kept sliding right up on him. It was just like he had lost his engine. I thought I was going to run into him. I thought, "I've got to get underneath him where he can't see me if I pass him."

So I ducked down underneath his airplane, continuing to slow down. When I got up to the front and pulled off to the right-hand side, I looked back to see that he had ejected. So I eagerly started calling "Ed," but I got no answer—didn't hear anything. I thought, "Oh, no! They got Ed while I was getting the guy that was after Ed. The guy that was after me must have got Ed."

Well, that wasn't the case. I kept looking around. I looked for fires on the ground to see if Ed's airplane had crashed. I called and called and couldn't find him.

While I was looking on the ground for fires, I get this call: "Tiger lead, Tiger two. Transmitting in the blind. My instruments are all gone. My engine's running but I don't know how much fuel I've got. I've been hit bad. I'm going to Choto Island and eject there." I thought, "Thank God he's okay."

So I headed for Choto Island and went over to Guard channel and the rescue aircraft. They had a helicopter stationed there, and they were airborne and heard that we were coming in. When I went on Guard channel, I heard them talking. They had Ed in sight. He ejected, and they went right along off to one side and went right down with him when he got in the water. They picked him up just within seconds—I guess thirty seconds or a minute in the water—and they were right there and got him. So, I came on home.

That was my fifth MiG, but when I got on the ground, my gun camera had not taken a single picture. Not one picture. No confirmation. My wingman didn't see it. There were no other planes in the sky. So I went in and I told them in debriefing what happened. They had no confirmation. The army Intelligence officer—a pretty sharp troop—said, "I'm going to Seoul tomorrow. Just sit tight. I'll see what I can do."

Four days later, on the twenty-sixth of November, he came back, walked in, and said, "I've got your confirmation." They have ways; he wouldn't tell me what he did, but I learned later that we had monitors who monitored all the radio frequencies. My assumption is that he went up to Seoul and checked the tapes. The MiG must have said that his airplane had been hit and that he was going to eject, which he did. He must have broadcast it under their frequency, and our monitors on

the radio channels must have picked that up. Other
than that, I don't know how he could have gotten confirmation. But I had my fifth MiG!

Another pilot, Captain Robinson Risner, who joined the
fray at nearly the same time as Foster, found that though
the combat was tough, there were times when the F-86
truly did outclass the MiG and almost made the job easy.

General Robinson Risner (eight kills)
18th Fighter Wing (recce), 4th Fighter Wing,
336th Squadron (after first ten missions)

Flying the F-86

I flew seven hours and thirty minutes in the F-86, and
they said, "You're combat ready." And I felt that was
the finest little airplane I've ever flown—the F-86. I'd
had a lot of fighter time, so it didn't take long—it was
such an honest airplane. There's hardly anything that I
can think of that you could do to get in trouble in it.

First Kill and the F-86

My first kill was done at a full stall. We saw some
MiGs below us, and that was unusual. To that date I
had not seen any below me; they were always above.
So I thought it might be a trap. As I committed myself,
I said to my number three man, who was my element

leader, "Check four, bogies is high." And he said, "We've got six more at three o'clock and they're coming in two by two."

So we were just a target, and they were coming in like they were practicing gunnery. So now that we were warned, as they came in we'd break hard into them. They were going much faster, of course, since they came down from about 2,000 or 3,000 feet above us. But they couldn't turn as hard as we could, so they would overshoot us, then just keep going and head for the Yalu River.

So when the last two had committed, I remember telling my wingman, "Get ready, I'm going to reverse on these two." I almost called it too close. I wanted to make sure I reversed in time to get behind them before they got out of gun range. And when I reversed, I was so close I could see the rivets on their tails. I unloaded a good burst on the number four man, and he pulled into a tight-climbing turn—a chandelle.

What I didn't know was that I had knocked his engine out with my first burst. First thing I knew, I was running up on top of him, so I threw the speed brakes out and chopped the throttle. Next thing, he starts falling off to the left, and I start shuddering.

I went into a full stall.

I thought, "Yeah, I guess I'm in trouble." But I had so much confidence in that little airplane [the F-86], I thought to myself, "You know, I might just feed left rudder into it and pull the gunsight right through him." He was already starting into a left spin. And, sure enough, in that little airplane, although it was in full stall, I fed the left rudder until I pulled the gunsight right through him.

I was holding the trigger down, and six .50-calibers were going. I chopped his vertical stabilizer off right against his fuselage. He bailed out immediately. So I got my first kill in a full stall. Confidence in the airplane after—well, there wasn't anything that I would sell it short on.

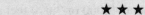

On September 21, a couple of weeks after Foster's exhausting encounter, Risner dropped a MiG for his fifth kill and would eventually go on to eight victories, honing his skills for an encounter that would be the stuff of legend and raise the question of just who the enemy was.

13

HONCHOS AND JUMPING THE BORDER

Throughout the war it was whispered about, but security concerns, worry about public opinion at home and, most of all, the fear of the conflict in Korea exploding into a far wider conflict kept the tale under wraps.

With the transfer of hundreds of Russian MiGs to the Chinese for the 1951 buildup, Sabre pilots were soon reporting that something didn't seem quite right. A handful of planes out of the swarms of hundreds were always in the thick of things whenever there was an encounter. Often bearing distinctive markings, these aircraft were handled with a superior skill, making them stand out like a race car driver zooming through a traffic jam of blue-haired ladies.

Rumors began to circulate about these "Honchos," as they were quickly nicknamed, the most prevalent one being that they were Russian master pilots, undoubtedly veterans of World War II, sent in to train the Chinese and North Koreans and to lead them into combat. There were even stories that a couple of them might be old American "China Hands," who at the end of World War II stayed on in the Orient and became mercenaries with Mao's army.

By this stage in the war, in spite of the vastly superior numbers and performance of the MiGs, kill ratios were approaching eight to one for the Sabres. The efforts of men like Blesse were finally taking hold as improved training programs, along with upgrades of the F-86, started to make a profound difference from the dark days of mid- and late 1951.

Most of these kills were clearly the result of superior piloting and tactics. Sabre pilots were increasingly disdainful of the skill of the average MiG pilot, who too often made some critical mistake in the first couple of moves. As Blesse and others pointed out, a dogfight was now a question of teamwork and instant foresight as to what had to be done next.

Working in teams, the leader moved in for the kill while the wingman devoted his attention to observing the more general situation and provided warning if something dangerous was coming up. Too often the Chinese formations broke apart, and once culled out, a lone enemy fighter was a sitting target.

As to foresight, the aerial encounters were an intricate three-dimensional ballet or game of chess, the key difference being, of course, that in the end someone usually wound up dead. It was not simply a question of making a maneuver, then firing; it was usually a battle of anticipations, the making of a move, the anticipation of what an opponent would do, then your countermove, followed by their countermove, then the final move, which was the checkmate.

Compounding this were the closing speeds, which often approached 20 miles a minute, weather, altitude, handling characteristics, and, of course, the boundary lines of the playing field. Regarding the Chinese and North Korean pilots at this stage of the war, it was generally acknowledged that they came into combat with a fairly good level of training, at times even superior training, but as a whole they lacked the imaginative skills demonstrated by a certain few who clearly stood out on the other side.

An enemy who broke the mold and who seemed to be one step ahead thus was an anomaly. These anomalies gave our pilots the ultimate challenge, and in the process usually wound up killing or dropping some of our pilots in nearly every encounter, creating speculation as to their identity.

Throughout 1952 at debriefing sessions, Sabre pilots repeatedly speculated that they had had a run-in with a Honcho. Some of this might be attributed to the fact that American pilots could not fully believe that there might be Chinese pilots out there with skill levels approaching their own. But there was enough evidence coming in to indicate that Russians were indeed taking part in the fight.

One pilot found himself in a wild dogfight where he and his opponent started into a series of barrel rolls, the two planes flying canopy-to-canopy over each other. The pilot looked up at his opponent, just feet away, and clearly saw a Caucasian face looking back. Several pilots reported pulling alongside a stricken opponent's plane and seeing a non-Asian pilot staring back, or circling in around an enemy drifting down on a parachute, noting that the pilot was blond, or redheaded.

An incident that carried with it the potential for exploding into a world war happened on November 18, 1952. Task Force 77, operating off the east coast of

Korea, launched an air assault against the town of Hoeryong, just across the border from the Soviet Union.

Radar picked up a swarm of fighters coming out from Vladivostok and heading straight for the fleet. Three navy Panthers from the carrier *Oriskany* went up to block them. A dogfight ensued over the Sea of Japan, and one of the MiGs was destroyed. The others broke off and headed back into Soviet airspace.

The incident was immediately communicated up to the Joint Chiefs and for several hours there was outright concern that this attack was a precursor of a general Soviet air strike against the task force. No more sorties came up, the task force withdrew from its close approach to Soviet waters, and the decision was made to classify the entire incident. No one knows if this Soviet attack was ordered directly by the Kremlin, or if it was simply an overreaction on the part of a local commander. Either way it was an encounter that yet again demonstrated the dangers of the Korean conflict spinning out of control.

After the collapse of the Soviet Union in 1991, evidence was allowed to surface that dozens of Russian pilots had indeed served in Korea. Their initial mission was to train Chinese pilots during the big buildup of 1951, and they often were the leaders of the Big Wing formations that loitered over the Yalu.

Like Risner—for that matter, like most fighter pilots of the time—a professional challenge could not be passed up and the Russians were as eager to test their skills, as were Hot Shots like Risner and Pancho Pasqualicchio, who had cruised up to the Yalu in a P-51 with the full intention of finding a MiG and bringing it down.

When the opportunity presented itself, Honchos would seek out a tangle with a Sabre.

Long after the war Risner actually met a Honcho. Though the passage of time had softened the rivalry, there were still some differences of opinion and of memory regarding what happened in the dangerous skies of MiG Alley.

General Robinson Risner

Honchos

I met a Russian pilot at a reunion who was a retired colonel. He claimed twenty-nine airplanes over Korea. You see, the Russians were not supposed to be fighting over in Korea. It's known now that they did. And this pilot flew his missions over Korea.

Some of the planes he claimed were prop jobs, maybe spotter planes and what have you, but I'm not at all sure that his claim of twenty-nine was verified. Anyway, we were discussing the attributes of the MiG versus the F-86, and I said that I was quite aware that they could out-climb us. They had superior combat training, and I emphasized the next when I said (through the translator), "And you could out*run* us!" I wanted him to know that they were more into running; we did the chasing.

So I said, "Anytime we got you below twenty thousand feet, you'd run." Now, I don't know how the translator translated that statement, but the pilot got a little bit haughty and said, "We didn't fight below twenty thousand feet."

I said, "How do you account for the eight-to-one kill ratio?" He replied, "You have your statistics wrong. It was eight-to-one in *our* favor."

And I said, "No, you're absolutely wrong."

We continued and were discussing the period of time he had been there and the period of time I'd been there. We found that he was flying over Korea at the same time I was. So he asked me, "Do you think our paths ever crossed over North Korea?"

I said, "No way." He asked, "Why not?" I replied, "If we had, you wouldn't be here."

Risner would go on to a final score of eight kills. He believes that a number of his subsequent encounters involved Honchos as well. His career with the air force would continue through the Vietnam War, and he would eventually rise to the rank of general.

14

1953: WINDING DOWN

By the end of 1952, Korea had become the "Forgotten War." Pilots returning home, once they stepped outside the circle of their military family, found that the attention of the American public had turned to other pursuits. The economy was still in its postwar boom (post–World War II, that is); if there was a focus on military matters it was over the escalating threat of a thermonuclear holocaust now that both sides had developed the dreaded hydrogen bomb.

The "wastage" rate on the ground front had simmered down to a slow but steady bleeding, with enough body bags coming home each week to cause some notice, but not enough to generate widespread public outrage. Eisenhower had run on the vague pledge of having a plan to end the war quickly, but negotiations would continue to drag on for six more months after his inauguration.

The old routine of missions continued. Directly over the front lines, tactical support units rained down napalm, fragmentation, and high explosives. On the long supply routes back up to Manchuria and Russia, interdiction raids continued. Bridges were dropped, only to be rebuilt in a matter of days and then dropped again. Hundreds of miles of railroad track were shredded and continually replaced by hundreds of thousands of laborers and over MiG Alley. "Big Wing" formations of MiGs still formed up north of the border, swept in above the ceiling of the Sabres, circled about and, when the opportunity presented itself, pounced down for a tangle.

In the waning days of the conflict, Colonel Harold Fischer would discover just how dangerous the war could still be. He had already served one tour of duty in an aging P-80, then was dragooned into serving as a pilot for a British general until he finally wangled a seat in an F-86 and was back in Korea. He ran up a remarkable record of ten kills in just seventy missions, an almost unprecedented ratio of one confirmed hit for every seven times aloft.

For Fischer, however, his aggressive drive would result in the war becoming a personal conflict that would last for two additional years after the armistice was signed.

With his fifth kill Fischer found as well the frightful human side of the conflict.

Colonel Harold Fischer (double ace, ten kills) 51st Fighter Group

My fifth kill came sooner than I expected and with it a great deal of trepidation and mental anguish. I have never been able to hate an individual of the enemy, but I could hate the ideology that controlled him and in which they believed. Consequently, I could fight well against the ideology that was threatening our system and way of life, but man to man, I could feel compassion. This fact was brought pointedly to view on my forty-seventh mission.

On this day our flight had been again scrambled on a search mission. The only way to conserve fuel in the search area was to climb to altitude, then let down; consequently our flight went to 40,000 feet. The ground controller, who had been silent after we had checked in with him, suddenly came on the air and told us to take up a heading due west.

We were over the Chongchon area, about 100 miles south of the Yalu River, progressing up to a point about 25 miles from the Chinese border to see if it would be possible to find the remains of an airplane that had been reported down. Another flight from the other squadron was proceeding north with us at a different altitude, when we received the word to turn to 270 degrees.

The controller was so precise that it was remarkable. He must have been one of the very best available. He stated that the enemy would be at our altitude 15 miles ahead and he was setting us up for an interception. Having little faith in the usual instructions, his very words inspired confidence. To my amazement, four dots rapidly became larger and merged into a flight of four MiGs on a southerly heading. It was a perfect vector and the only one that I received while engaged in the Korean air war.

There were four aircraft heading south. Our flight set up an interception turn, and we fell in behind them. It was perfect: four aircraft behind four others. If we were lucky, everyone would take home a kill. Just as we were ready to fire, the MiGs utilized their favorite tactic—they zoomed for altitude. As they began to go up, the number two man evidently panicked, and his aircraft wings rocked back and forth. Apparently he either could not continue the climb or he chose what to him might have been a more logical action. Three aircraft went up, and the fourth went down. I fell in behind the fourth and ended up about 4,000 feet behind him.

Looking through my gunsight, he appeared too far away for the radar gunsight to operate. So the logical action was to again turn it off and use a fixed gunsight. There was only one thing to do and, squeezing off short bursts at the aircraft, I hoped to slow him down so that I could join up with him and finish off the encounter. Judging what I thought would be the proper elevation for the range, I fired a few rounds spasmodically. This went on for a long time, without any indication that I was hitting the other aircraft. Once a spark lit up on the aircraft ahead, and I called out to the wingman that I had finally hit him.

There were only two of us now, since the other element had attempted to follow the other three aircraft. For what seemed like an agonizing period of time, my aircraft gradually drew nearer to the MiG. We had been in a slanting dive for miles and were well into the northern reaches of China now. There was no one else around except the two of us at a lower altitude and the element leader hovering at high altitude clearing my aircraft. It was an eerie situation.

Gradually a light began to grow in the tail of the MiG ahead of me. First a small pinpoint of light developed, like a candle lit on a dark night. Then it grew until it enveloped the entire tail of the aircraft. By the time that I drew within ideal range, there was no need for me to expend ammunition.

It was a dying aircraft.

The rate of closure was fast, and the entire fuselage was a flame holder for the now desperately burning aircraft. Rather than fire on the aircraft again, I pulled up alongside to look at it. I wish I had not. The pilot was beating on the canopy, trying to escape.

The heat must have been insufferable, since the canopy was changing color and the smoke was intense. Up to that moment, the enemy had been impersonal—each aircraft a target that had little meaning and not associated with flesh and blood. But the sight of another man trapped in the cockpit of a burning aircraft with no power and no place to land was a psychological fact impossible for me to forget.

Seeing me, the pilot attempted to turn his aircraft and evidently ram me. It was easy for me to evade him by moving out to the side. There was only one thing for me to do; to put the pilot out of his misery as quickly as possible. Sliding behind the MiG, the molten metal of his airplane came over mine like a light rain shower and partially obscured my windshield. I pulled up the nose to fire and squeezed off a few short rounds.

Like Captain Risner and others, Fischer also had his run-ins with the legendary Honchos. On April 7, 1953, Fischer apparently encountered a Honcho, triggering a series of events that would eventually lead him into an extended stay north of the Yalu River.

Honchos

One of the most interesting speculations of the war was whether we were fighting Oriental or Caucasian pilots. Further impetus was given to these speculations by the fact that one of the pilots had damaged an aircraft and, seeing that it was helpless, he had moved up to the side of the airplane to look at the pilot, who had not bailed out. The pilot had jettisoned his canopy, so our pilot was able to look very closely at the other man in the airplane. He stated that the pilot was large, had red hair, was definitely not Oriental, and shook his fist at the victor.

This lent credence to the report that there were other than Orientals flying the MiG and other aircraft. We even speculated that there would be Americans who had been with the Chinese and were flying with them and against us. This rumor was buoyed by some of the pilots who had been flying in the Far East at the end of World War II and who had been offered money to fly for the Communists. Speculation was that they were still being paid by the Chinese or that they actually believed in what they were fighting for.

Another fact the pilots were concerned with was that there seemed to be a great deal of disparity in the performance of the pilots encountered in the Korean air war. Some were excellent, and some were novices. There were a few pilots of the enemy forces who would abandon the airplane immediately when fired upon. This occurred, it seemed, whether or not the airplane was hit by enemy fire. Flights that were afflicted with the apparent malady were called "jackpot" flights. In some cases, these individuals would take no evasive action whatsoever when fired upon and continued to fly straight and level, with another airplane firing at them from the six o'clock position at the ideal range.

Then there were the apparent masters of the game.

When a pilot came in contact with them, they would usually be doing the firing and, when they were attacked, you were lucky if you were able to make a mark.

Several pilots returned literally white with fear from encounters with these superior pilots. A good friend of mine had one on his tail. He literally did everything in the book to evade, and the only thing that he could finally do was to put his airplane into a violent forward spin and hold it until he reached lower altitude. When he did this, he had to spin through a literal barrage of cannonfire, and he was lucky that he did not accidentally hit some of it.

One experience with a master pilot came on a very memorable mission. Our job was to patrol the Chongchon River, and the patrol was from the mouth of the river to a point about 100 miles inland. We set up a sausage-shaped patrol and edged our aircraft higher. Also, our aircraft made their turns so that increasingly our flight path came closer to the Yalu River and "MiG Alley," the place so familiar to the readers of the newspapers back home.

The controller kept calling our flights back to the patrol area, and we would grudgingly come back to the intended part of the patrol. This tug-of-war went on for what seemed an undeterminable period of time. My position was over the entrance to the Chongchon River, and the other flight was positioned at the other end of the orbit.

Without warning from ground control, the other flight began to call out bogies. Suddenly they were also calling breaks. A decision had to be made whether to progress to the scene of the battle or to wait for them to complete their sweep, which would bring them into my flight's area. As soon as the information came over the radio, the element leader departed, leaving me with my wingman.

Climbing as high as I could, I turned the flight to the east, hoping the MiGs would come underneath me to the right and 90 degrees to my course. For once, like the books say, the planning paid off.

A flight appeared from the right, then another, and the last flight came right underneath me. Choosing the number four man, who passed under me, I turned left and dropped down line abreast with him—only a few hundred feet separating us. It was an ideal situation and an excellent opportunity for the dogfight of World War I. No matter who won this encounter, it would be a fight to remember.

In the best traditions of Mannock, Udet, Bishop, Nungesser, and the heroes of the World War I dogfight, the situation unfolded. Immediately both of us started to scissor, each trying to get on the other's tail by turning into and then away from each other. The flight paths of both our aircraft resembled an interlacing pattern. For a few moments, the situation was static, with neither side having an advantage, then I took a calculated risk.

One of the things a pilot theoretically should not do is to drop his speed brakes. This would reduce his speed, and speed could always be converted into altitude. The one that had the altitude had the advantage. But this situation could go on longer than I liked, since there were so many other aircraft in the area.

Dropping the speed brakes for a short period of time, my airplane fell behind the MiG. Seeing that the advantage was on my side, the MiG headed for the border just a few miles away. His aircraft was forming heavy contrails, and I was 600 feet behind him. The contrails were so heavy that when I pulled up to shoot, my canopy entered his contrails. The radar gunsight was working marvelously, and the first burst of a few seconds caused his aircraft to light up almost from wingtip to wingtip. It seemed that every round found its mark. Before I had a chance to fire again, the canopy went by, followed by the pilot. My wingman verified the kill immediately for number one of the day.

I looked over to see my wingman's position. He was off to my left and slightly higher. Looking at him and at the MiGs in front of us, I saw him fire, and the right wingroot of the MiG sparkled with an excellent hit. It was his first mission deep in enemy territory, and it was already a success. Before he had a chance to press his advantage, we turned and he called on me to break, since I had a MiG on my tail ready to fire.

Looking over my shoulder, a shiver of fear coursed through my frame. There, about 1,500 feet out at seven o'clock position, was a single MiG. I recalled the tales of the professionals who flew alone. Rolling up and over, I pulled as many inverted Gs as I could without stalling the aircraft and losing my airspeed.

Doing a split "S," I called again, although it was hard for me to talk with the force of the Gs pressing my body to the seat. I asked if the MiG was still there. My wingman called and stated that he wasn't there the last time he saw me, but that he had lost me and was heading home. Checking my own tail, I set course for the front lines.

Going North

Continuing our flight northward alone, I saw a flight of four aircraft come across the border, pulling contrails.

Positioning my element above as they passed 2,000 feet below us, we attacked. As we gained our position, the flight began to zoom.

Before they had the advantage, I fired my guns. At 1,000 feet they were off 200 feet to the right. This was because I was flying an aircraft that had not been bore-sighted from the mission before. It was organizational policy to bore-sight the aircraft after every mission when the guns were fired. The aircraft was given to me because there were no spares, and there was no one to blame but myself, since I had accepted it. The only thing I could do was curse, which I did vehemently.

Before I could correct for this error in the guns by adjusting my sight pattern, we were attacked by four following aircraft above the contrail level. There was nothing we could do but to break off the attack. It was not a break in the true sense of the word, but it was a turn and a reversal of the turn, so now we were again the attackers. But it was no use; the aircraft were traveling too fast. Rather than pursue the issue, which was hopeless, we set up our course for the mouth of the Yalu and then home again.

My wingman evidently had a tip tank that had not fed, because he called that he was getting low on fuel. At this time three aircraft came across our noses, heading north. It was an ideal situation. I called a bounce and my wingman called that his fuel was getting lower. I made the wrong decision, telling him to head out and I would follow him as I had done before.

I continued the attack. There were three aircraft, one straggler behind the two in front. Choosing the straggler, I dropped down and closed with him at a tremendous rate of speed. Getting off a shot, I made a gigantic roll around him, then fell behind him. The MiG in front accelerated and was now even with the other element, which I was rapidly overtaking. I rolled over on the number two MiG in the formation, and this time my guns were calibrated. I let him have a long burst and stopped his engine.

He dropped back, giving me an opportunity to hit the lead aircraft. From about 1,200 feet, all six .50s literally tore the aircraft apart. Debris came back by my aircraft in large pieces, and I unconsciously ducked as pieces went by. There were two choices: either to go down under the MiG or go over it. I decided to go over the airplane, because I did not want to be in front of the MiG as I had been one time before.

At this time the throttle came back into my hand, the engine instruments read that I had a dying engine on my hands, and my speed began to decelerate so rapidly that I was pushed forward against my shoulder straps. I thought of calling, but did not, because it might have been interpreted as a cry for help.

The mouth of the Yalu was possible to reach, but I determined that I would be at zero altitude and the characteristics of the F-86 in ditching were not predictable. If you hit just right, the plane would not immediately go under, but the chances for this were slight. I decided to risk it until I smelled that bane of all pilots and saw smoke issuing into the cockpit . . . fire!

Now there was no decision to make if I wanted to live, for the aircraft would probably blow up within a very short period of time. I had to bail out. Reaching down for the left handle, I jettisoned the canopy. With the right handle pulled up, I leaned back in the seat, put my feet in the stirrups, and squeezed the trigger. The altitude was 2,000 feet and the airspeed 450 knots.

Prisoner of War

The 37-millimeter shell that activated the seat gave me a terrific impetus upward. It caused me to momentarily black out and, when I recovered, the first indication was a rushing of wind around me as I rotated rapidly in space. Immediately pulling the ripcord, I waited for the tremendous opening shock that I expected. There was none, and this came to me as a great surprise. I had followed all the procedures that had been rehearsed. First you unstrap your safety belt, then you push away from the seat, and the last action is the pulling of the ripcord. When the parachute opened, the first indication was a slight jar. Then I looked up and checked the panels. They were all there save one.

Looking around for other aircraft in the vicinity, I saw a MiG that was a derelict in the sky. It was trailing a long stream of flame, as long as the fuselage. It turned lazily toward me and I thought it would fire upon me. The only thing I had was my chrome-plated .45, otherwise I was defenseless. But the MiG turned just as lazily away from me, and I turned my attention to landing. The MiG was one of those that I had fired upon, and the pilot must certainly have had a desire for revenge. Fortunately, he did not pursue it.

The terrain below me was rocky and hilly with scrub brush and trees growing on the side of the rocky crags. Where to land was a problem as I gradually drifted toward the side of a small hill. I was certain that I was going to break my leg at least on landing. The stillness around me was surprising, and I could hear voices on the ground shouting. They seemed to come from all directions.

The second surprise that occurred was the landing. Expecting that at the very least I would break a leg, I literally drifted down, and my landing was cushioned when the canopy of the parachute caught in the branches of a scrub tree. This saved me from a bad landing and roll down the hill. Releasing the harness of the parachute, I lay back a moment and evaluated the situation.

On my scarf I saw a lot of blood, which blended into the yellow cloth. Looking around to see where the blood came from, I gingerly felt my ear. Evidently when the helmet came off, it had torn my ear and caused it to bleed. My body was completely soaked with sweat, although it was fairly cold, and a feeling of complete tiredness came over me. I attempted to climb up the hill, but I could not get up.

The only way I could move up was to crawl. I checked my watch and found out it was 5:20 P.M. If I could hide until dark, there was a possibility that I could elude the pursuers, whom I could hear all around me.

Dropping my life vest, I began to move away from the vicinity. Before I left I dragged my parachute down from the small tree so that it would not be visible to those who would soon be seeking me. I still had my chrome-plated handgun. Moving from the crest of the ridge where I landed, I started to crawl to get away from the general vicinity.

Crossing a small ravine, I approached the crest of the hill adjacent to the hill where I landed. If there were someplace to hide, I would have dug myself into the side of the hill, but there was no place. I was going to cross over the crest of the hill when I heard voices on the other side. Deciding to wait, I crouched down just below the crest of the hill and waited.

Soon a small, dark Chinese dressed in typical farmer's attire came down the ravine from whence I had come. He was unarmed and reminded me of a farmer that was out trying to track a lost cow or horse that had strayed. I had my .45 in my hand, and there was no cause for concern, because he posed no threat to me that I could see. I had heard that there were many friendly agents in this area, and the thought went through my mind that perhaps this individual was a friend and not an enemy.

He came up to within 20 feet of me before he saw me, and then he gave no indication of surprise. He made some motions, and instantly making a decision, I decided that he must be a friendly agent who could lead me to shelter. Putting all my trust in him, I followed him down the ravine. He in no way indicated that he was anything other than friendly to me. At the bottom of the ravine, we were suddenly confronted with a large group of peasants carrying every type of agricultural tool imaginable and a few old rifles. I had had it.

The group of about thirty Asians milled around me and inspected me as if I were a creature from another planet. They were not in any way hostile and, after taking away my weapon, which I secreted in my immersion suit, they directed me to a small hut, which was close by the bottom of the ravine. In it they directed me to lie down and rest, and I saw evidence of confusion among them. Was I an American or another of the white pilots that were evidently flying from their bases?

A plan formed based upon this indecision. I would make it as plain as I could that I wanted to go to the nearest air base, which was just a few miles away. Getting up, I started to walk in that direction. When they protested I insisted in my language of sign and word. Using this strategy, I was able to move ahead down the road and position myself about 50 or 60 feet ahead of the group. The usual number of children followed closer than the adults. I thought about running, but the immersion suit that I was still wearing precluded this.

Another group of what looked like militia then approached, and there was an argument between the civilians and the militia. The civilians wanted me to go in the direction of the airfield, and the militia wanted me to go the other way. Both began to push with me in the center and, for a moment, the issue was debated more violently than I desired.

When one of the militia—evidently the leader—secured some wire, I thought that I was going to be strung up immediately. So I acquiesced and sat down by the side of the road. By this time there were two guards with rifles who were uncomfortably close. Escape was now a thing of the past.

Soon a jeep came roaring up the road. It was the standard military model used by our forces, and four Chinese soldiers were driving it. With more force than was necessary I was placed in the backseat or, rather, tossed into it. Turning around, the jeep began to carry me toward the airfield that I was headed for originally. About a mile further, the road was blocked by the remains of my aircraft. The last time I saw the plane, it was circling around me and disappeared behind the hill. There in front of me lay the remains of about $700,000 that was now merely scrap.

As the jeep stopped, a soldier who was evidently Russian came up alongside of the vehicle. This individual was immensely hostile. Behind him I could see a Russian truck and four other Russian soldiers loading the scrap on a truck. I foolishly had some identification with me, and this evidently had been reported to him, because he came up to me and, with the four Chinese soldiers holding me down, he took the identification. I have never seen so much hate in an individual as I saw in this one. I was glad that the encounter was so brief, for we immediately moved around the wreck of the aircraft and went directly to a small village.

The small village must have been the headquarters of the Chinese army in this area. None of the soldiers wore stars on their cap, so they were eventually destined for the Korean theater. Stopping the vehicle, the four guards took me into what was evidently a large meeting hall.

I was placed in the center of the room on a chair, which rested on a dirt floor. At one end of the room, there was a telephone, which was probably being used to determine just what to do with me. All around me, peering in the windows and in the doors, were Chinese soldiers of all shapes and sizes.

One of the soldiers who was braver than the rest brought my portable oxygen cylinder to me and attempted to ask me just what it was for. I pulled the activating pin and he almost dropped from fright. He made frantic attempts to shut it off, but to no avail. I also saw my .45 on the hip of a Chinese, who probably was very proud of the weapon.

After innumerable telephone calls, a squad of Chinese indicated that I was to go with them, and we went out the door to another American army vehicle, a carryall. There, squeezed in between two soldiers, we went to various villages, where the population viewed the American pilot who had been shot down. Conspicuous among these villages were the youth groups, the pioneers. Already I was a political prisoner.

The eventual destination was the airfield I had attempted to reach. I wanted to reach it for two reasons: one was that if I could convince the Chinese that I was a MiG pilot, I might have been able to escape and, secondly, I had no desire to be a prisoner of a hostile, ungoverned mob.

Entering the confines of a large barracks area, I was blindfolded and taken to a large building. I was immediately placed in the dormitory. Many soldiers in nondescript uniforms were lying on beds or sitting at tables in the dormitory. One of the individuals, who seemed to be in charge, indicated to me that food was available and also that I would not be shot. This was somewhat of a relief to me.

One individual who could speak a little English asked me the number of my airplane. I had no idea what the number was and, when they insisted, I gave them a number that satisfied them. The food arrived shortly thereafter and it was an omelet, which, even under these circumstances, tasted very good. Whenever I turned around, there were individuals looking in the windows. Finally, the windows had to be covered up.

After what seemed like a long time, another individual came in and asked me to take off my undershirt. I did this with the assistance of the guard, then I put it back on. I had no idea why they did this except to see whether or not I was armed. After he departed, I was taken across the street or driveway and put in a room with a bunk.

The soldier or airman on the top bunk sleepily woke up, then went right back to bed. I was given a blanket and told to go to bed. A guard sat up on a chair in the middle of the room. You would think that it would be impossible to sleep under these circumstances, but sleep can be a repression in many circumstances, and so it was in this one.

Early the next morning, four o'clock by my watch, four soldiers came into the room and woke me up. I stumbled to my feet not knowing where I was. The horrible reality was almost too much. I was taken out to a truck with an open bed and forced to lie down in it face down. A rough ride ensued.

Lying face down with my eyes closed, the ride over the rough roads was almost intolerable. Two soldiers rode in front of the truck and two were on duty in back, guarding me. After at least four hours, a guard stopped the truck, and we drove up to a barracks-type building. Here my blindfold was taken off, and I was introduced to the place where I was to remain for a week while they decided what to do with me.

Before arriving at this area, which I estimated was about 15 miles from the border, I was not interrogated very extensively, just asked a few questions. But now the real interrogations began and continued intermittently for the next twenty-seven months.

There were about ten barracks-type buildings that were situated in the valley formed by two low ridge-lines. It was evidently a training ground area for troops being sent to Korea. Half of the barracks buildings were two-story, and the other were single-story administration buildings or, as I found out later, latrines for the troops. I was taken to the second floor of one of the buildings where a squad of soldiers was located and placed in a small room that must have been used at one time as a storeroom. There was nothing in the room except a bare floor with a board over it, which was to be my bed.

As soon as I arrived and was taken into the room, the interrogations began. A tall Chinese came in and introduced himself in the normal western manner. He said that I should call him Lou. By way of introduction, he said that he had been a flyer with Chiang Kai-shek and that he had been trained in the United States at Luke Field in Arizona. He had flown the P-47 and had fought against the Communists for a long while and had eventually deserted. He joined the Communists while he was staying with some relatives and had been with them ever since.

He was personable and probably the best interrogator that the Chinese had at the front. He interrogated other prisoners, I found out later, and seemed to be the one that initially was used to soften up the prisoners or to assess the approach that was to be used to gain the results they desired with each prisoner.

He asked me if I was hurt or if I needed anything, then said that I did not have to worry about being killed. He stressed the lenient policy that was followed by the Chinese People's Liberation Army. He mentioned that if I cooperated there was a possibility that I could return home and asked me if I remembered that, at the beginning of hostilities, some American prisoners had been released right after they had been captured.

Then he stated that my crime was very serious, that I was guilty of violating the sacred territorial air of China. This I certainly could not refute. He stated that I was not to be blamed for these actions, that it was the aggressive United States policy, and those people who formulated the policy were to blame. When I asked him what was expected of me and what was going to happen to me, he said that depended upon my cooperation and asked me if I knew about the germ bombs that our forces had dropped on their country and that of Korea. In this setting our preliminary sparring was over and the interrogation began.

An hour after Lou left, there were a lot of footsteps on the stairs, and each individual looked in the small confined area where I was kept without even a chair to sit on. A scraping of chairs and talking in Chinese indicated they were planning their approach and asking themselves what their actions and attitude should be.

Then I was summoned into their presence. Walking up to what I assumed was their leader, I saluted, but it was ignored. I was told to sit down by the interpreter, Lou. While they had been planning their approach, I had been planning my reaction to their interrogation. I adopted the attitude that I was uninformed, naïve, and rather surprised at the benevolence of my hosts. The latter was certainly true, for they were acting very differently from how I believed they would act.

However, there was nothing in my past that prepared me for what was in store for me.

I decided that I could tell them what I thought they knew and to act dumb on things that were sensitive. This gave me a great deal of leeway to use my judgment. The questioning began: name, rank, serial number, organization. What was I doing in China? Did I know where I was? Who were the pilots with whom I flew? When I did not answer, they told me. I originally began to tell them of the pilots that I had flown with in the 8th Fighter-Bomber Wing, giving them their names as pilots in the 51st. They let me go on, then told me of the pilots in the 51st.

This immediately gave me new insight into their Intelligence system, and I hoped that we had one as effective as theirs. Interspersed with military questions, there were personal questions and questions about my lifestyle. As time went on, I found that they would question answers that were truthful and accept as fact for the moment answers that were fictitious.

All this was interspersed with threats, veiled promises, friendliness, and coercion. I fully expected physical violence to be unleashed upon me at any moment despite the repeated statement that "We do not harm our prisoners."

This interrogation ended on a very bad note, as it was intended to, and I was ordered to write down the layout of our base. This I refused to do. I was also to list all the pilots in the organization. It was the end of round one.

Later an individual who evidently was the political commissar came in and lectured me concerning the great benefits to China that resulted from the Communist revolution. It was interesting that even during the interrogations, I would be subject to these political lectures.

Occasionally Lou would drop over to voice superficial concern over my welfare and treatment. It was damnably cold during the nights, and when I complained about the clothes I had, he stated that he would try to get me some warm winter clothes. He emphasized that it was not easy to supply the prisoners with clothes. Food was another matter of concern, since there was very little that I could eat of the Chinese food that would satisfy me. The Chinese continually stated that the POW camps in Korea were ideal, that the troops there were given special food and ate better than their Chinese guards. I certainly could believe it, since I ate with the squad of soldiers whose food was adequate for the Chinese but certainly not for the western individual.

When asked what I desired, the first thing that I could think of were books. I indicated that I was interested in learning as much as possible about China, which I truly was. The first book that was given to me was *Yo Banfa,* written by an Australian who had established a colony of a type in China. It was interesting though badly written, but it did pass the time. When they found out that I was interested in books, they used this as a reward or punishment, either by withholding or giving books to me. What would be done with me was still unknown to me and, to the day that I left, I held the desire and partial conviction that I would go to a Korean prisoner-of-war camp.

On one of the days that I was there, Lou informed me that there was going to be a treat for supper. The squad that I was a ward of did its own cooking, and one afternoon everyone came back early from their duties and made the equivalent of meat dumplings, which they called *jowtszas*. Even though this was supposedly a delicacy, it held very little appeal for me. If I had known what would occur later as far as the food situation was concerned, I would have eaten much more.

Going to the latrine was an experience. It was a community affair in a long, low building. Instead of stalls normally found in latrines, it was entirely open, and the repository was a hole in the cement about 8 by 24 inches. It reminded me of the facilities found on some of the farms before inside toilets were convenient. Whenever I went to the latrine, which was a considerable distance away from the barracks, I often saw two soldiers in another barracks. When they saw me, one stood on the lower level and the other on the upper. As a joke the one on the upper held a rope, which was around the neck of the one on the lower. Needless to say, this was bad for my morale.

Escape is always in a prisoner's mind, and it was no less in mine. I found that it was particularly strong in the early stages of captivity, and my mind ceaselessly searched for an avenue of escape. In fact, the only reason that I can determine why the attempt was not made was that the end of the war could be tomorrow, and there was the possibility of going to a Korean prisoner-of-war camp where I could converse with my fellow Americans.

There is a vast line between thought and action as far as the average prisoner is concerned. The prisoner's thoughts are always on escape and home, and each new situation is assessed according to its merits and in light of his feelings. Many times I thought that a person could do this or that if he only dared and, with audacity, could easily achieve success. It seems the desire to escape looms largest when the prisoner is initially captured and dwindles when he has grown accustomed to his surroundings.

Further, a prisoner and a guard can never be friends unless there are some unusual circumstances in the situation. Their desires and purposes are directly opposed, for one desires freedom and the other has the directed mission of preventing this freedom.

The day arrived for my departure from this environment. With no warning, I was told to bring along what little was given to me (soap, toothbrush, toothpaste, and a small towel). Then I was taken to a room where a large number of people were crowded in, perhaps fifty or more. At one end of the room sat a Chinese official with an interpreter, and in front of him were two others in blue uniforms with movie cameras. Many thoughts went through my mind as I tried to imagine what was going to happen. The situation looked favorable, since if this interview or interrogation was to be filmed, it would act as a record of sorts and someone might see it and know that I was alive. No word of my end could possibly have reached our sources at this time, although I told the Chinese that I had broadcast that I was going to bail out before I departed the aircraft.

I was seated with the Chinese official at my right and the interpreter at my left. Then the Chinese began to tell me basically what I had heard during the past interrogations. The Chinese People's Liberation Army had a lenient policy concerning prisoners: I would go home when the war was over, for there was no reason to keep me; that violating the Chinese territorial air was a serious crime and I was personally not held responsible for the aggressive actions of the Wall Street warmongers. During this time the cameras ground away and the people intently watched and listened. I listened, since there is always a faint glimmer of hope that actions such as these might result in freedom by some miracle of great magnitude.

Immediately after the interview, I was taken out to another of Uncle Sam's jeeps. Four Chinese soldiers, whom I had never seen before, escorted me. I was placed in the backseat with two individuals, and a towel was wrapped around my head so that I could observe nothing. There were two Chinese soldiers in the front seat. All of these soldiers had on red stars, so they were not members of the Chinese People's Volunteer group; they were the People's Liberation Army troops. [Throughout the Korean War, China maintained the legal fiction that all of its troops serving in North Korea were "volunteers," and that therefore China as a nation was not actually involved in the conflict. Therefore, Chinese troops serving in Korea did not wear the insignia and unit patches of the People's Liberation Army.] This should have given me an indication of where I was going, but hope springs eternal in the human breast.

15

THE LONG EXILE

Colonel Fischer's saga was not over with his transfer out of a holding area. Rather than being sent to South Korea, he was shipped north by train. His testimony, published here for the first time, stands unique as the record of a POW who had been left behind.

To Mukden, China

The thought that this train might be going to Korea was dispelled by the fact that our air cover allowed nothing to move once it crossed the Yalu River, and the Yalu River bridge was a nightly target of the B-29s ever since they canceled the day missions. About three o'clock in the afternoon, the train moved south and gave me another twinge of hope, but it was only to load at the station.

About 50 percent of the train where I was located was filled with passengers—men, women, and children. My heart hit the bottom when it finally started its trek north-ward in daylight. Where was I going? Was I going to disappear into the vast reaches of China, never to be found or returned? Was I going to join the vast hordes of slave labor that the Communists were reputed to hold? All these questions rapidly followed one another in my mind. When the train moved away from the station, I had only the guards with me on the hard seats of the train. At each stop of the train at the small villages, more Chinese would get on the train until it was full by western standards. Dozing off on the seat, I awoke with a jolt and thought that I was in Bedlam. I was squeezed into a corner and there were Chinese all around me.

For a moment I felt like screaming to relieve the tension. The heat and the pressure were stifling, and to add to the confusion, a Chinese was haranguing about some subject, which I was sure was whether to hang me now or later. An official of what I thought was the railroad police came and allowed him to talk, but controlled him to a certain extent. How I would have liked to have been able to understand Chinese.

The train continued for what seemed an endless period of time, when it finally approached a large city. The train pulled up to the depot and we got out after all the other passengers left. Then, with a guard on each side of me and one in front, we proceeded to a new small Russian automobile. It was here that I was able to see a sign, with the name in Russian, which I was able to determine was Mukden. This city was about 100 miles in the interior of China, and at one time was a thriving industrial area of importance under the Japanese.

As we drove to the outskirts of the city, I passed a factory that I remembered seeing in a *National Geographic* magazine published after the war. It showed an aircraft factory that was producing biplane aircraft for the Japanese army, and when World War II ended, the Communists had stripped all the machinery from the plant and taken it to Russia. This picture and article made an impression on me, and I recalled it as we drove by it. Shortly after passing this old factory, which still had some motor mounts stacked beside it, we pulled up to what had been a factory of some type. A guard opened the gate and we drove into what was to be my home for the next two years, except for a very short period of time when I made an escape.

The Russian automobile drove up to this structure, the main purpose of which was probably light industry with an auxiliary or allied function of making bricks. A door at the side of the building facing east was the main entrance, and around this door were soldiers of the People's Liberation Army basking in the early morning sun. Through this door I was taken into a dim hallway, which was cold and almost damp.

Stopping before a large door, I made my entrance into a very large room that reminded me of a converted granary storage area. The ceiling was high, and at the far end of the room, opposite the door, were two windows that were about six feet from the floor. Around these windows were boards on the inside that did not permit one to see out unless he suspended himself from the ledge and raised himself up or used something to stand on. There was nothing in the room either to sleep or to sit on. This was my home, and I was in complete solitary confinement.

I looked at the room, its size and coldness, and I have never felt lonelier in my life. Later a blue steel cot was brought in with a straw mattress. This was all the furniture that I was to have for a long time.

Cold was to be a factor in my imprisonment, and even when it was warm on the outside, the rooms were like a basement. It was almost impossible to get warm with the little activity that was permitted me. The guard soon brought me a bowl, which was to be used to relieve myself. Since all conversations were in Chinese, it was impossible to understand exactly what was expected of me. When I used the crockery bowl to relieve my stomach condition, I found that it was to be used for a urinal only. If one wanted to defecate, he had to ask the guard, and if there was another guard available, the prisoner would be escorted down to the end of the hallway that ran in front of the cells to a long latrine. The latrine was similar to the one that was used at the camp where I was held prior to coming to Mukden, except here there were stalls. Prisoners were not allowed to have such luxury as privacy and the guards would hold the door open to see if we actually did what we had asked to do.

At first it was impossible, no matter how bad my stomach cramps were, to relieve myself with someone watching the operation. One guard was so avid in doing his duty that he would crouch down to see if the prisoner was successful. If a prisoner could not do what he had asked to do under the circumstances, he was told that he was *poor how,* which was the opposite of *ding how,* or very bad. This word was used more than any other that I can recall while in China. It was to be used with various emphasis of severity during almost every phase of the imprisonment in China.

All the actions of the prisoners had to be learned from bitter experience, since there were no rules given to the prisoners, and they were under the complete direction of the guards, who spoke only Chinese. Under these conditions the prisoners picked up the language very rapidly.

When I was initially escorted to the latrine, one guard would go ahead and close the little sliding panels in the doors, where our food was served. This alerted me to the fact that there must have been other prisoners whom I should not see or who should not see me. When the meals were brought, the guards would go to great lengths to hide the fact that there was someone further down the hall or that there were stops prior to reaching my cell. With such pains taken to conceal the fact that there were other prisoners, it seemed very important for me to make contact with them, both for their safety and mine and to relieve myself of the driving, compelling loneliness. So, since escape was always in my mind, it would have to be accomplished with someone else in order for it to be successful.

The opportunity came sooner than I had expected. In the evening prior to going to bed, a guard who liked to talk to the prisoners was on the shift. He was young and evidently had a desire to learn the language, and he would come to the doors and attempt to use his language ability and improve it with the prisoners. He stopped at my door and peered in the cell. He wanted me to write down my name on a piece of paper, which I was glad to do. After I had done this, he asked me how to pronounce it. This was a contact that I thought might give me some information or perhaps could be bribed to do something for me. I asked in sign and word to find out the name of the person in the next cell.

When he hesitated I offered him the only thing that I had that was valuable—a pair of Marine Corps flying gloves I had been able to retain. Offering him these gloves, he hesitatingly went over to the next cell, and I could hear the conversation that was going on. The prisoner was reluctant to speak loudly, and I could barely hear what he was saying, but his name did come through. It gave me a great shock, for it was someone I knew whom I had thought was dead. The name that I heard was Andrew Mackenzie, Squadron Leader, Royal Canadian Air Force.

It was impossible to contain my excitement, and I called out to ask if he had a glass eye. He responded with a yes, and it seemed almost as if it were a miracle. This was a pilot that everyone thought was dead, and here he was, alive. Andy's glass eye was a positive veri-fication. He had picked it up from a friend of his when he was flying Spitfires from England during the big has-sle. His friend had gotten it from a London lady of the night, who took it out at night when she pursued her business. Andy kept it as a souvenir and good luck charm. When he'd had a few at the bar, he would sud-denly turn his head, and when he looked around again, he'd have this protruding eyeball in place. It was an item of conversation and a trademark, so to speak, of Andy's.

When I called out, the guard immediately came to the door and indicated that I should be quiet. Because he was doing me a favor, it was the only thing I could do. By talking to him, I was able to get a piece of paper from the other prisoners with their names on it and to give them mine. This was more or less mutual protec-tion, because it would lessen the possibility that one of us could be done away with if we made known that we knew that others existed in this building.

The other two prisoners were Ronald Parks and Lyle Cameron. Ron had been with the 51st Fighter Intercept Wing and had gotten lost after he had been hit. He had flown into China following what he thought was the coast of Korea. He had finally bailed out over Port Arthur, which the Russians held and where there was an airfield.

So there were four of us in the cell block, with someone occupying the fifth cell in the row but with whom Andy was unable to make contact. It was difficult to make contact with Lyle and Ron, since there was a partial divider in the hallway, and the acoustics were such that it was virtually impossible to talk to them without shouting. However, when the guard was down the hall, Andy and I could talk to each other with little cause for concern.

Contacts were necessarily clandestine and of short duration. Because of this, it was decided that we should make contact some other way. Our cells were dirty, so we decided to ask the guard for a straw broom, which was kept in the hall. One of us would ask for the broom, and after he was finished, he would secrete a message in the handle and give it to the guard. After a period of time, the other prisoner would ask for the broom to clean his cell. In this way Andy and I kept in contact for a period of time, and I was briefed on how Andy had been captured, what the daily interrogations were about, and how he had been treated.

Andy told me of his last mission. He and his wingman had made an attack on some aircraft and were pulling away when he was hit. His aircraft began an uncontrollable roll, since evidently his hydraulic controls had been damaged. There was only one thing he could do, and that was to bail out. He pulled the handles on the ejection seat and, as he separated from the seat and pulled the ripcord, an F-86 went by him. He was convinced that an F-86 had shot him down and, although he tried to view this objectively, he was nevertheless a little bitter about the incident.

After separating from the seat and pulling the ripcord, he drifted down and landed on the side of a hill about a mile and one half south of the Yalu River. North Korean soldiers had evidently been following his descent, because a truckload of them stopped a short distance away from him and began to pursue him. He ran to the top of the ridge, and the soldiers fired on him. Soldiers were running up the other side, and there was no place to go. The only alternative was to give up, so he did.

After his capture, he was taken across the river into Manchuria, and though he was blindfolded, he still detected the river crossing. There he met the same Chinese man who greeted me, Lou. After a short interrogation, he was taken back to Korea, where his serious interrogation began. He was very brusque and military at first, giving only his name, rank, and serial number and demanding to be shot if that was to be his fate. He kept this up for about two weeks, when the Chinese came through with information about his old squadron in England and those in it, as well as information concerning the 51st Fighter Intercept Wing. This caused him to contemplate his position, and to offer some information. This evidently impressed the Chinese in charge, who indicated that Andy would soon find himself in a North Korean prisoner-of-war camp. However, he made one mistake.

Where Andy was being kept there were other prisoners that had been shot down. Included in this group that Andy had contact with was a B-29 tailgunner. One evening Andy was talking clandestinely with the gunner, and he stated that he wanted to escape. They were planning the initial move, when the interpreter who had been covertly listening, walked up to the gunner's window and asked him if Andy had been talking about escaping. In his frustration, the gunner said yes. Within a few hours, Andy was in a jeep and again taken across the Yalu River. He was driven all the way to Mukden without his blindfold being taken off. He had no idea where he was, and when I told him that he was being held in China, he could hardly believe it. All the time, his interrogator had told him that he was still in Korea. He had been in this cell block ever since.

Andy's main concern was his wife and whether or not she knew that he was alive. She was a very beautiful woman, and Andy wondered if she would marry if she thought he was dead. It was a very disconcerting situation, and in solitary confinement one is not always rational, which the Communists well knew.

After an initial settling down and before he becomes accustomed to the prison routine, the prisoner's existence for the first thirty days is a nightmare. During the first thirty days, there is a great deal of adjustment that must take place before a prisoner realizes that it may take time before he is released and will not, unless he is tremendously lucky, go home tomorrow. During the first few weeks at Mukden, when the time grew heavy, I actually counted the minutes. To make them go faster, I would see how long I could hold my breath. Under these circumstances, the prisoner wonders whether he will be killed or released.

The Geneva Convention on the treatment of prisoners of war has nothing to do with these circumstances. Realistically speaking, prisoners are a lost cause for the side that loses control over them and a liability for those that capture them. Realizing this, the normal prisoner will often wonder why he has been spared when so many of his friends have been killed. He will also wonder if he did the right thing when he bailed out or surrendered. He will go over the alternatives a million times in his mind. In my own mind, I thought of whether I should have stayed with the aircraft and risked ditching it in the mouth of the Yalu or whether what I did was the only alternative. Andy debated whether or not he could have rolled all the way to the offshore island or whether he did what he had to do. At the time the action is taken, there is no doubt that anyone given time to think over the situation will certainly have doubts, particularly when he has a great deal of time to debate the pros and cons. A prisoner exhibits paranoiac thinking in solitary confinement.

Interrogations began seriously when I arrived at Mukden. They could be classed as military, political, and social interrogations. Sometimes they would be interspersed with all three types. At times it was even difficult to determine whether it was an interrogation at all or whether it was merely a question-and-answer session. It became evident that there was not a question about anything concerning the military that we were not supposed to know. "I do not know" was not accepted, and this led to fictitious answers. Soon it became apparent that to get the Chinese to believe anything, you had to tell the same lie three times at three different interrogations.

During the interrogations the prisoner was cajoled and threatened with both direct and indirect threats. At the cessation of the interrogation, the prisoner was asked to write down various answers to the subject or subjects covered that day. The first subject I was faced with was my relatives and what they did. Included in this was the desire to determine how much money they made annually. Recalling the words of the Intelligence officer with the 80th Fighter-Bomber Squadron, I made my entire family from a proletariat background, which was easy, since they were. Both Andy and I wondered what would have happened to us if we had relatives on Wall Street.

One of the interrogators was a Chinese man who had picked me up at the camp near Antung. I did not know that he spoke English until we were near the end of our long train ride, and I never expected to see him again. But he was the first Chinese to enter the door of my cell as an official interrogator. He was small and rather sickly looking, and his eyes were dilated. The first thought I had concerning this individual was that he was a dope addict. When he came into the cell, he had such an arrogant air that I almost felt like killing him and, for a moment, irrationality got the better of me. Then I thought that he must be a very brave man to come into a prisoner's cell like this without a weapon and face a man who had been an enemy but a few days before. His attitude was such that he would have been hated anywhere. His name was Chong, and he would be with us for the full two years or more that we remained in this environment.

Gradually the days began to blend into one another. The words that characterized this imprisonment were "lenient policy of the Chinese People's Liberation Army"; "violated the sacred territorial air of China and must be punished"; "war criminals"; "Chinese people desire that you should return home"; "Your case is different"; "Wall Street warmongers"; and "Have faith in the Chinese people."

The food began to have its effect, and my weight dropped down until, looking at my legs one morning, I began to feel as if I was an atrocity case that I had seen pictures of during the end of the Third Reich. Sleeping was impossible at first, and I could never seem to get enough of it, particularly at the beginning when the lights that were on all the time had to be grown accustomed to. Sleep loss, tension, and weight loss all played a part in the physical and mental deterioration that occurred during the initial phases of the internment.

And into this environment were fed, in careful measured doses, clever propaganda of a theoretical nature that fell upon a susceptible mind. This idea of the world revolution for the proletariat was something that was new to all of us and just what we had been taught to hate and what we were all fighting against. In my conversations with Andy, I noticed that he had been influenced by the information that had been given him and the talks that he had with the interpreter. But this was nothing against Andy or the rest of us, for we were highly susceptible from our physical condition and tension. We were all just following the application of sound, explainable, psychological principles.

Another interpreter besides the one that had picked me up was soon assigned to us. He had evidently just been assigned to the unit as an interpreter. He was very young and wore a blue uniform, which indicated that he was evidently not a member of the army but perhaps a type of civil service worker. He was largely assigned the task of our political education officer, and he would have long talks, in his own way, with us, concerning our political thoughts.

You had to be very careful what you said. It developed into a game of thinking what the other wanted you to think, to guess his thoughts and to attempt to keep your thoughts to yourself. Sometimes these play actions were too much, and you had to voice your opinion. When you did voice your true opinion, then you were guilty of reactionary thoughts. The paradox was that the interpreter encouraged us to speak our thoughts, to say what was on our minds so that he could trap us more easily. We were being conditioned.

The Chinese made a planned effort to constantly manipulate the environment that we found ourselves in. After a period of time, we were able to find out when an interrogation was being scheduled for us. At this time the food would become significantly better and there would be small improvements in our daily living. This could mean that a prisoner would receive additional food of some nature, tobacco, or books, or some little amenity that would give him encouragement. In this way the prisoner was properly conditioned to the new meeting, which was certain to be forthcoming.

At times the other prisoners would receive this bonus effect and you never knew just who would be picked for interrogation. The grapevine was working well at this stage of the game, and we were able to pass on all types of information about what the interrogator stated to whom and what the interrogations were about.

Normally, the way contact would be made was the way that seemed most easy. One of the prisoners would get the guard engaged in some activity, either talking or asking him to accompany him to the latrine. Sometimes the guard would allow the prisoner to go without the aid of another guard, and for this short period of time, many words would flow back and forth between the prisoners—two would talk and one would listen. It was interesting to analyze what the interrogators would tell each prisoner, for they would tell one prisoner one thing and another just the opposite. It was in this crazy penal world that we found ourselves.

The days were good or bad depending upon two factors that seemed to be entirely unrelated. If the sun shone, my spirits were high; when the weather was bad, it was very difficult to keep significantly high spirits. The other factor was the attitude of the interpreter. If he indicated that perhaps we would be going home soon, then my outlook was bright and, conversely, when the interrogator mentioned that we were considered war criminals, my spirits hit bottom. There seemed to be no normal day. You were either elated or dejected, and the swings could occur within a very short amount of time.

Food was something that occupied our thoughts. The diet of rice or unleavened bread, interspersed with vegetables in season, was hardly the proper diet for a man who was accustomed to meat, potatoes, bread, milk, coffee, and dessert. Consequently, much of our thoughts were occupied with food that we had eaten and food that we would eat in the future. One evening I was walking around the cell and imagining that I was eating apple pie. The illusion was so real that I actually visualized it in my hand and I began snapping at it like a dog gulping down food. The guard looked in and told me to be quiet, for evidently the snapping of my teeth was distracting to him.

Five days a week we were served three meals a day, and on the remaining two days only two. However, the noon meal left much to be desired, usually consisting of rice gruel or a little rice and preserved turnips to season the rice with. Occasionally on the holidays, there would be very good food. Always enjoying good Chinese food, it was doubly appreciated when it was served under these circumstances. It was a rare occasion when the stomach could be full and satisfied. To get over the craving pangs, I would literally stuff myself with rice, of which you could have all you wanted. Five minutes later, it seemed, the hunger pangs would return.

What to do with the spare time that was forced upon us was a serious problem. At first, the only thing you could do was think and hope. Gradually, as your horizons narrowed to the confines of your cell, you would begin to look for amusement within the cell. The shapes on the wall of the cell would be studied and your imagination could picture all sorts of shapes and memories from these stimulants. Truly your life is lived over from the first memories to the latest. As each phase of an individual's life is lived over, he may dwell on a particular portion for literally days before he passes on to another.

Sadly, a large portion of time is spent feeling sorry for yourself and thinking of the alternatives to the major decisions made in your life. A great deal of self-analysis is undertaken by all prisoners under the circumstances. I thought about my parents, girlfriends, cars, farms, college, flying training in the utmost intimate details. Under the circumstances, sex—normally a tremendous motivator—became less and less of a motivator and gave less and less trouble as time went on and only the memory remained. Poor food was also a factor in the diminution of drive.

Rationality was not always with me under the circumstances of being a prisoner. At one time I gave vent to my rage against the injustice and frustration of being a prisoner and shouted and ranted at the guards, kicking the door of the cell and calling the Chinese every name in the book with the majority picked up from my short naval career. I made no attempt to control myself. This brought a number of guards down the hall, and I was escorted to a cell away from my own block. Here I walked around the cell, threatening everyone and everything. Finally rationality returned, and I was as peaceful and serene as if all my troubles were suddenly washed away. I felt a little sheepish at letting myself go like that.

I was taken before what was then the commandant of the camp, a large Chinese man who looked like one of my Indian countrymen. He always seemed like he was on the side of the prisoner. In any case, he was always smiling, which helped, because I would rather be shot by someone smiling than someone who was always scowling, although the end result is the same. The Chief, as we called him, sentenced me to be placed in a small back room that I was to know later for another infringement. In this room there was not even a bed, nothing but a solid floor of poor concrete.

Here I spent three days, which to me seemed longer. Along with this confinement, I also had to write myself criticism for the actions and promise not to do them again. This was a clever move from a psychological standpoint, since it put the prisoner on the defensive, and he never knew exactly how many incidents could be placed against his name and put him on the list of nonrepatriates. This was their most effective threat.

As a prisoner's horizons narrow, he turns to what is in his immediate range of attention. In my case there were spiders to study as they built their webs and caught flies. I had one particular spider that would weave a web in one corner of the cell, and when I had fed him five flies, he would move. Soon his web would appear in a new location. Five more flies and he would move.

In my youth I built gliders from balsawood. In China this hobby of my childhood came forth, and the guards used to give me empty matchboxes. Taking the matchboxes apart, I was able to build small gliders, which I flew around the cell. This was a source of my own amusement and that of my guards. A deck of cards was given to me, and I literally wore the cards to tatters playing solitaire. I had all but forgotten the rules, so I made up my own. Through playing solitaire, I was able to determine the probability of beating the game. For every fourteen attempts, I was able to beat it once, using the system that I devised.

For a month I played at least eight hours a day with the cards—they were that welcome. Also as an indication of the lenient policy of the Chinese People's Liberation Army in respect to prisoners, I was given a set of paints and paper upon which to draw designs and pictures. Always having the desire but not the talent for the arts, this gave me an outlet but no satisfaction with my meager abilities. Using rice paste, I had the entire cell ringed with pictures of flowers, landscapes, and anything that caught my fancy. All of these things were outlets and helped to pass the time of day, for which I was grateful.

Because we were getting pale and asked for some fresh air and exercise, we were allowed to go outside in a small courtyard that was adjacent to our cells. Here we could enjoy a little piece of blue sky and some sunshine if the hours were right. It was also an opportunity to wash our clothes, which needed it very badly. By this time we were all wearing padded clothing, which after two or three months began to stand up by themselves as the guard pounded on the door to get us up. But they were warm, and on the times that we were allowed out, we could wash them.

July 1953 rolled around, and the guards had been indicating that there was very little fighting and then that the fighting had stopped. This was what we were waiting for, because our captors stated that first the war had to be over and then our case could be discussed. With the approaching end of hostilities, our treatment began to improve. The first concrete illustration of this was the fact that a club room was opened up for the prisoners. Evidently there were a number of prisoners who used this club room, because we were allowed only about fifteen to twenty minutes at a time, in a small room that had an accordion, violin, Chinese checkers, some magazines, and an old Victrola.

One of the treasures of this club room was some old V disks that had been cut during World War II and released to the troops. On the V disks was inscribed: COMPANY G, 2ND BATTALION OF THE UNITED STATES MARINES STATIONED AT TSING TAO. Duke Ellington was featured on one side and, for a moment, I could close my eyes and be back listening to the greatest again, if only for a moment. The emotional impact of these moments was hallucinatory and very unreal. To find World War II disks in 1953, from a marine unit stationed at a Chinese port, evidently after the end of World War II—what a history those records might have told.

Comradeship

The interpreter finally did come in and tell us that the war was over. He told Lyle, Ron, and me this, but when I checked with Andy, they had told him that hostilities were still going on. This was a shock. Why should they tell three individuals one thing and lie to another? Just what was the truth, and what ends would they achieve by not telling the truth? This was a perplexing situation, so after the interpreter came in and told me the war was over, the next day I told him that I did not believe him.

In my short experience with the Chinese, I found they never desired you to have too much of anything, whether it was food, hope, or despair, so when I acted very dejected and stated that the war could not be over, a clipping in the paper was finally brought in and shown to me. There were the officials of both sides meeting at Kaesong and signing the truce agreement. After this I was convinced. Clandestinely talking to Andy, I convinced him, but we both were unable to determine why he had been given the wrong information. This worried all of us. It was something that we could not figure out.

Everything had been going very smoothly. The guards had been given instructions to be friendly, though sometimes their instructions were to the contrary to aid interrogations. Our food improved, but our political indoctrination continued. At one time we had more books than we could read, which was a miracle in itself. All this culminated in an event that all of us were waiting for, and when it happened, we were overjoyed. It was an event that was to again strain our emotional pendulum to the upper reaches.

I was taken to a room where I had often been interrogated. This time I noticed that the guards were smiling. At the time I had no idea what was going to happen. Entering the room, I saw a full entourage of Chinese facing me. The first words that were interpreted were, "Your request has been answered; you may now live with other prisoners." And with these words Lyle Cameron was ushered into the room and introduced. Lyle was tall, blond, and about twenty-five years old. He was dressed as we all were, in blue padded clothing. After being introduced, we were told to sit down, and Ronald Parks came in and was introduced to me. Ron was short and wiry. Ron and Lyle had been together at another place. Everyone was all smiles and happy to be together, to see someone from his own land. This event was the highlight of our stay at Mukden.

We went back to Ron's old cell, and there we had three beds and three writing desks moved into the big room. It did not seem like the same cell that I had been in just a few minutes before. There were so many words that each of us wanted to say that it was impossible to mouth them fast enough. There had been so much unsaid during those short, clandestine meetings when the guard's attention was diverted that it was almost painful now. As a result, only the most important subjects were discussed.

It turned out that all of us were from the Midwest— Lyle from Lincoln, Nebraska, and Ron from Omaha, Nebraska. My own home, where my parents still lived, was Sioux City, Iowa. We were all in an area that was not over 300 miles away from each other, so we each knew a little about the general locality of the other. There was much to discuss, and we had a lot in common. The time passed fast when the three of us were together, and there weren't enough hours in the day to talk. The guards would knock on the wall and door to signify that we should be quiet after dark. It was interesting to talk about how we actually fell victims of fate and how we happened to be here in China. If we'd had an idea of what was in store for us when we left the paternal protection, we probably would not have left.

Lyle had been flying F-84s and he was based at Taegu in central South Korea. On a mission there was a lot of fog and early morning mist in the area, and they let down from altitude over what they thought was their intended target. Locating a train, they dive-bombed it, getting excellent hits. Lyle with his second bomb concentrated on the target did not notice that he was too close to the target and not far away from the lead aircraft.

The bomb from the aircraft ahead of him exploded, and a fragment from it struck his aircraft in the right wing. It immediately started to burn and, at low altitude, he did not have a chance. The fire curled around the wing and began to eat away the main airfoil; Lyle had no choice but to bail out. On the way down, the flight circled around him, then left. Lyle landed close to the train, which had been used to haul wounded Chinese volunteers from the front. Later he found out that the train he had attacked was not in North Korea but in China. There had been a serious miscalculation in the navigation.

He was immediately captured by the soldiers in the train and tied up. As he was tied up, one of the railroad workers came up to him with a hammer used to tap the junction boxes of the railroad cars. It was sharp and, when used as a weapon, very deadly. The railroad worker raised the weapon, and Lyle thought that he had "bought the farm." Fortunately the railroad worker was only threatening, and Lyle had a new lease on life. After this he was forced to walk among the wounded soldiers as they spat on him—a humiliating and degrading experience.

Ron had a somewhat different experience. He was in a fight near the Yalu River, and after damaging another aircraft, his aircraft had been hit. They had been below the overcast, and when he climbed up, he was disoriented, since his instruments had been damaged. He followed the coast of China, thinking it was the coast of Korea. When he ran out of gas, he glided down. Under him was an airfield, cleverly camouflaged. In fact, he saw aircraft landing and taking off in and around what were apparently stacked cornstalks. As dusk was gathering, he bailed out.

Landing on the side of a hill, he proceeded down a small path and ran into an old Chinese man. He threatened him with a pistol and forced him, he thought, to take him to some food and shelter. The old man obeyed, but under different circumstances than Ron had imagined. He was led to the center of the village, and when the old man saw another group, he screeched like a plucked chicken and warned all the Chinese villagers. Before Ron knew what had happened, the local "mayor" had him on a platform and was lecturing the peasants on an evidently sensitive subject. Ron thought he was about to be hung. Soon the Russians took him into custody. The area was under their protectorate. While with the Russians, he had been well treated and fed, but he was turned over to the Chinese after a few days' interrogation.

Ron was shot down sometime in September of 1952 and was taken to a Chinese prison somewhere in Mukden, where Chinese Nationalists and Japanese prisoners were still being held from World War II. He was there about a month and a more lonely situation I could not imagine. Then in October, Lyle arrived and the cadre of American prisoners in this situation was increased by 100 percent.

The day Lyle and Ron were actually allowed to be placed together was probably one of the great occasions for both of their existences in China. For here were two Americans being held prisoner in northeast

China, young and unmarried, and placed in a Chinese prison. The emotional shock of having to endure this existence must have been tremendous.

Their tales of living with the Chinese prisoners were both hilarious and sad. Both had suffered initially from severe cases of diarrhea, and they were fortunate that they had access to a private latrine, because even the few steps to the commode were filled with extreme hazard. They told of prisoners in shackles and of prisoners not being able to move except when the guard told them to. The prisoners had to sit facing the door all day and could not move unless the guard gave them permission. One of the prisoners evidently went out of his mind. He screamed twenty-four hours a day and was heavily shackled. Only the very mentally stable would have been able to endure such deprivation and misery, although there was no evidence of physical punishment.

Ron and Lyle were together from October 1952 until April 1953, when they were separated and brought down to this prison where we met. They had been in solitary confinement from April until July, when the three of us were placed together. The primary concern of all of us now that we were together was what was going to happen to Andrew Mackenzie.

The main thing on our minds was the fact that Andy had not been told of the end of the war, and now he was not the fourth man in our unit. What were they going to do with him now that we had lost contact with him? After a month had elapsed since we had lost contact with Andy, we decided to do something about the situation. We all got together and decided we would tell the Chinese what we knew of our Canadian friend. This was not a decision that was easy to make, because we realized there were certain perils involved, but it was difficult to see how they could punish all of us, so we decided to make it a group venture. It was interesting to note the reaction that occurred.

When the interpreter came in the next day (incidentally, it happened to be a new one who had recently arrived), we told him about the prisoner down the hall. He flatly denied that there was a prisoner there, then asked us to write what we knew of the prisoner. I wrote it down, explaining how we knew that he existed and what we knew about him. The repercussions were quick to occur. Later that same day, I was taken from the cell and placed before a panel of officers and interpreters.

The atmosphere when I walked in was grim and determined, and I could see that it would come to no good end for me. I was told that I was an activist and sentenced to be separated again from my compatriots. Taken to the same room to which I had been sentenced before, I was placed in the same circumstances. Thinking that I might be in for a little longer period of time than before, I settled down to a waiting game that I thought would never end.

At the end of the week, I expected to be released, but instead I received a bed. At the end of the month, still in solitary, I received a desk. The time was late September 1953, and some of the prisoners were being repatriated. The first group had gone home, and there awaited the next group that would go the same month. And still nothing happened.

The routine of interrogations was stepped up, and the questions now concerned border violations. They wanted precise details on when crossings were made, at what altitude, and how many aircraft. This I had no way of knowing, and they knew this, but the pretense of credibility had to be made, so I lied for peace of mind. When I told the same lie three times, they believed it no matter how ridiculous it seemed. But in the evening, I would have to go over the things that I had said, because I knew that I would be asked about them again.

Of concern to all of us were the germ-bomb accusations. They seemed silly when we first heard of them, but the interrogators actually gave a credible pretense of believing them. There was a great deal of semiofficial literature supporting the contention of biologic warfare, which the common people might have believed when it was put out by their government. I was asked about this information, and in order to relieve the tension, made up a story so fantastic that it was a release of tension just to make it up.

Both the Chinese interrogator, Chong, and I knew that this was a fantastic lie, but to save face, the farce had to proceed. I made up the operation code name of "duress," which meant not that it was a code name but that this information was given under force. Once I gave it the name and repeated it three times, it became official. Then quite elaborate details were gone into, such as creating a special oxygen system for the bacteria so that they would not perish at high altitude. Further, there had to be elaborate precautions to heat the projectile that housed the "germs." All in all, it was a story that would have thrilled the heart of a science fiction writer. Because I made it so detailed and fantastic, the Chinese could not refute it.

As the Christmas season drew near, I became very dejected and depressed, because here I was in solitary confinement—my seventh month alone with only myself and my thoughts. And no matter how many thoughts go through your mind under these circumstances, it is impossible to think of new subjects to debate after you have been in solitary confinement this long. As Christmas approached, a thought came into my mind. If I am not home or on my way home by Christmas, I'll attempt to escape. This thought became an obsession for me. The more I thought about it, the more my mind searched for a way that it could be accomplished.

I set a few criteria, one of which was that I would not hurt any guard and that I would attempt to get away without their knowledge. My scheme was aided and abetted when one day I picked up a nail while out in the sun for a short period of time. Secreting the nail in my pocket while the guard looked the other way, I began my plan. The cell that I was situated in was adjacent to the outside wall, and my bed was pushed up against this wall in the corner of the small room. There was barely enough room for the bed and desk alongside the wall where the door opened. I could take four steps one way before I had to turn around. Often I would spend hours pacing up and down the confines of the cell, like a caged animal.

Underneath the bed that abutted against the wall and under the small window, I began my escape attempt. Scratching the surface of the wall, I found that it was quite easy to scrape away the soft concrete, especially when I used the hot water that was always served us and threw it on the wall to let it soak. The time was January 2, 1954, when I began to remove the debris in earnest. I had to time my work under the bed when the guard was at the other end of the cell block.

During this time I was a model prisoner, smiling and being friendly to all the guards and thanking them for the water and food that they brought. Since I was so good, they never thought about coming into my room and checking it. If they had, they would have only had to raise the blanket that I let hang to the floor, and they would have found an increasingly large pile of debris that was accumulating from my constant chipping away at the wall of the cell. Many times the interpreter would come in and sit down on the edge of the bed. We would talk, and I would smile at the secret.

As the debris gradually accumulated under the bed, the tension mounted, because the danger of being found out grew with each particle of sand and brick. The walls of the prison were very cheaply constructed. There was a thin veneer of cement, then a tier of bricks, six inches of sand, and a layer of bricks that formed the outside wall. By constantly dousing the wall with water, it loosened the small amount of cement and sand that bound the bricks in place. It was a simple matter; however, it took a great deal of time to accomplish.

Finally there was only the outside layer of bricks that remained in place. I was very careful to loosen each brick just enough so that they would not fall out unless a slight amount of pressure was applied to them. When this was done, I had only to wait for the right time to accomplish the escape. I made the decision to wait until the weekend to make the big move. The reason for this was the fact that the guard seemed to be just a little more relaxed during this period, and the final exit would be easier.

The day finally came.

The weather was warm and balmy—much too warm for this time of the year. It was January 16, 1954, according to the calculations that I kept on my crude calendar. Only two meals were served on the weekends, and when the evening meal arrived, I secreted two loaves of the small bread that the Chinese were famous for in my blue jacket. It was best to hide these things on my person. Though the cells were searched, individuals rarely were.

Fortunately, there was no search while I made a very quick trip to the latrine and back. One of the guards was in my cell, but I returned so fast that it was impossible for him to make a thorough search. He sheepishly walked out of the cell as I turned the corner with my chamber pot, which I had emptied in the latrines. Waiting for the evening to arrive and the lights to go out, I thought again about the feasibility of escape and the plan that I would pursue.

It was foolish and foolhardy under the circumstances, but I felt that if I were ever going to return home, drastic measures were necessary. There was also the likelihood of a loss of mental stability. I began to hear a buzz in my ears that would not leave. At first, I thought that the Chinese had a radio station nearby, and I could hear the hum of the equipment, but when I questioned the Chinese, they emphatically denied the fact.

The plan that I decided to follow was to proceed to the airfield nearest our camp and attempt to steal an airplane. This was an idea born of desperation but one that was well worth the effort, since the distance I would have to travel was great. The second alternative was to try to board a train and travel either southeast to the Korean border or southwest to the port of Tientsin. Because of the climate, this was the way to travel. To attempt to walk under winter conditions in northern China would mean to invite defeat or incapacity in this unfriendly land.

But I had to escape. The die was cast, and not to escape at this time would have meant that a great deal of my time and effort would have been wasted. For a little freedom it would be worth it. I decided that the ten o'clock guard shift would be the one that I would access and make the final decision to move. The guard came on and by his footsteps and sounds, I could tell that he would rather be somewhere else than at the post guarding sleeping American prisoners. I piled some clothes in the bed to give the appearance that I was still in there, and I had already conditioned the guards that I would place my desk in front of the head of the bed, so that they could not see my face as I slept.

Slipping out of the bed and underneath the covers, I gingerly pushed out the bricks in the outer wall. Now there was no choice, I had to make my move. Pushing my heavy padded pants and jacket out the hole in the wall, I poked my head out of the building and breathed the fresh air of freedom. But something was wrong; the hole was not big enough. Panic overcame me. Then, thinking a moment, I turned around and put my feet out and by hunching my shoulders, I was able with a little extra effort to extract myself from my surroundings. Listening a moment, I realized that I was free, and the feeling was worth every effort that I had put into planning and anxiety.

Escape

It was a wonderful feeling to be free at last, and everything I had gone through made it worthwhile. Just prior to leaving, I left a note indicating that I had no intention of doing anyone bodily harm, since the possibility that this would be a successful junket did not loom large.

Gathering my clothing and moving to the side of the

building, I put on the heavy padded jacket and trousers. Then, adjusting a towel I had made in the form of a face mask, which Orientals used extensively when they had a cold, I started east across a small field used for tilling cabbage. It was the most direct route away from my place of confinement. Now I looked like any other Oriental and, even attempting to emulate their walk, I continued east to a small drainage ditch. Following this ditch, I headed south to a road that ran east and west.

As I came to the road, there was a Chinese soldier and a girl of the army sitting by the drainage ditch. It was fortunate that they had other things on their mind than investigating a rather tall "Chinese" proceeding at a rapid pace to the south. Coming to the road, there were a number of Chinese walking in both directions, and I moved over to the side of the road and walked with them, taking care never to be right in front of them too long. For maximum safety, the best position I found was to be either slightly behind a group of Chinese or well ahead.

I proceeded directly to what I thought was the airfield. The road I was following took me to another road, where a large group of Chinese were going south—the location of the airfield I desired to go to. The time was about 10:30 P.M., and it seemed as if this was a shift that was going to work at the airfield. My hopes rose, as this might give me the chance to get on the airfield. As our group approached the airfield, my hopes were dashed, because the Chinese had to pass through a checkpoint before they were allowed to go into the plant.

Continuing south past the main hangars, I noted that the entire area where the hangars were situated was closed in with a high fence. Logically concluding that this meant the airplanes were all inside the fence, I realized there would be no possibility for me to gain access to the airplanes unless I went over the fence. The difficulty would then lie in getting the airplane on the runway. It was a tough decision to make, but the only choice I had was to abandon the somewhat idealistic plan of stealing an airplane and take up my second alternative. With this in mind, I continued to where I thought the runway was and decided to cross this and continue southward to a railroad station. Before me was an open expanse of clear area, or so I thought.

I began to walk to the southeast, when out of the darkness loomed a guard, evidently from the airfield. Where he came from I had no idea. Coming directly up to me, he began to demand something of me in Chinese. There was nothing I could do but to indicate in Chinese that I wanted to cross the airfield. This I did with much gesticulating and vociferousness. When it became apparent that this one-sided discussion was getting us nowhere, I turned around and walked very rapidly back to the road from whence I came. He shouted at me and, although he had a weapon, he evidently had no intention of using it. At that time I would have kept right on going even though he fired, for the feeling of freedom was strong within me. The guard was evidently shouting for the man in charge, since a jeep soon came racing up. By this time I had reached the road and hoped that I had mingled with the Chinese. My blood was coursing through my veins from the close call and the excitement of the escape.

Ever since I had escaped, there were a great deal of white vehicles with red crosses that would come up and down the side and main streets with their sirens blaring. The blaring of sirens and appearance of the vehicles sent chills running up and down my spine, and the first chance that I saw to get away from the main stream of traffic, I took. It was a small alley running south on the very outskirts of Mukden. It led through a place where evidently the garlic was dumped, for the stench was terrific. The dogs from all these small houses, which were fenced, set up a terrific din when I came near.

Finally I was out in the country, and for all practical purposes I had escaped, because there was nothing south of me except open country that I could see. The weather was unseasonably warm, and this should have alerted me for what was to follow. In fact, my entire body was soaked with sweat from the physical and psychological strain. Continuing southeast on a heading of what I judged as 150 degrees, my spirits were at the highest. Everything was going as I had planned except for the brief disappointment at the airfield. Knowing where I was, the next obstacle to cross was the river that made a "Y" to the south of the city of Mukden. It was somewhere ahead, and at this time of year, it would present no problem in crossing. Surely in January it would be frozen.

Before I reached the river, I heard the sound of running water, and there in front of me was a wide expanse where the river had cut down into the level soil of this area of China. There was something wrong, because this river should have been frozen. I stood dumbfounded at the bank of the river and gazed across to the other side. There was ice at the periphery of the river, but in the center the water flowed dark and menacing.

My spirits dropped as I stood on the bank. There was no conceivable way that I could get across the

river without swimming, and to do this would invite
disaster even if I made it. I saw no way that I could
carry my clothes and my shoes across without getting
them wet. Instead, with a heavy heart, I headed south,
following the bank of the river.

A few miles south, there was a railroad bridge that
crossed the river. It was well lighted and guarded. Here
was a chance that presented itself that might get me on
the railroad cars and take me where I wanted to go.
Progressing inland, I crossed the rails and approached
the south side of the railroad bridge. Looking at the situation carefully, I determined that it would be impossible to find a spot on or in one of the rail cars. There
were spotlights on each side of the cars that illuminated the entire car. There was nothing to do but to proceed down the river and hope that somewhere there
would be a chance to cross.

With this new disappointment, I walked further
south and lay down by the side of the river to sleep for
a few hours. When I awoke, I was covered with frost
and hungry. Taking out the crusts of bread that I had, I
ate them and looked around for the snow that was to
furnish me with water. There was none, and this was
important, for a body has to have water in order to survive for an extended period of time. Arising, I walked
in the bright morning sun, past peasants who were going down the road in carts pulled by small horses that
looked too small for the job they had to do.

This road was too risky, so there was nothing for me
to do but to go back again to the riverbank. Following
the bank of the river until late in the afternoon, I finally
came to a point where it was possible to get across the
river without immersing myself. The only thing that
got wet was one of my boots, which I had cut off from

my survival suit. Crossing the river, which was little more than a stream, I made it over to the other side much later than I would have desired. In front of me were villages of brown dirt construction that interspersed fields tilled by Chinese for generations with very little change.

Over their fields had flown Japanese and American warplanes, and now Russian airplanes flew over their terrain to their base at Port Arthur. In front of me lay the railroad that I counted on, and there was nothing for me to do but to reach it and analyze the situation. Crossing through the fields, I skirted a village where the natives were threshing their grain. By now, hunger and cold were making their mark on me as well my lack of sleep.

I began to grow more tired as time went along until finally there was nothing for me to do but lie down and rest. One place that I rested was in an old gun emplacement that must have been put in China by the Japanese. It was now the second evening of the escape, and the weather was turning cold. The railroad was on my left and, with the coming of darkness, I would have to get to a village and attempt to get on the train going south. When I passed the village, I went back to the railroad and walked like an itinerant back home, down the middle of the tracks. I picked up orange peels and soy beans and placed them in my pocket for food that I would need later.

As darkness fell, I approached a small village. Having passed through a village before, I was able to determine that the trains would stop at every other village going one way, so it was necessary to travel to a village that was privileged to be on the list for a stop. This way each village had a train servicing it. However, if the citizenry of the village happened to wish to go the opposite way that the train went, they had to travel to another adjacent village on the rail line. I could make no real logical conclusion from all this, but it necessitated that I progress to the village that was fortunate enough to have the trains running south.

Moving south along the railroad, I found that each bridge had its guard on it, and this required my detouring around each bridge. Moving along the track, I suddenly heard sounds of gunfire and saw a peasant and his wife start up in terror and move the other way. Why this occurred I do not know, but it gave me a little hope that there might be friendly Chinese in the area. Then, approaching the village, I noticed a graveyard with the sign of the cross, and in the distance there was a steeple, indicating an attempt at Christianizing the population.

Coming down another path, I suddenly saw a white person, and both of us were so startled that I immediately moved on, attempting to ignore this startled look, for it meant only disclosure. Moving into the town, I crawled into a railroad coach to watch the rail traffic and determine when would be the best time to get on a train. The trains would come through and stop for a moment. If they were large and carried heavy loads, they would not stop. It was interesting to note that some of the equipment had evidently been used in Korea, for it was bullet riddled. Since it was almost nine months after the war, it might have suffered from guerrilla activity.

As darkness fell, I came out of my hiding place. It was cold, and I had no water. There was a little snow now out in the country, but it had been there for a long time. Dust and weed stems had blown into it, making it hard to swallow and giving little relief from the thirst that plagued me. I walked down the streets and saw the people eating in some establishments. I went to the door of a little shop and asked in Chinese for a drink of water. The keeper of the small grocery gave me a drink and, when I offered to give him my wristwatch for some food, he indicated that he was not interested in such a bargain. Rather than press this, I left and went again to the station where the Chinese were boarding small trains. They were packed, and, for a moment, I thought about getting on the roof of the train and riding along.

I was getting colder and weaker, and there was little hope left. I thought again about walking to the border of Korea, but this I deemed hopeless, for I did not have the energy for it. I was cold, hungry, and sick. The cold was a cube of ice in my stomach. It forced me to make a major decision. Either I could die out here in the cold steppes of China, or I could go to the warm station and ask for food, shelter, and warmth. There seemed to be no other choice for me as much as I desired that there should be.

Basically it was a question of survival and, whether an individual is in an airplane or on the ground, the will to survive is greater than the death instinct. The desire to live drove me to the railroad station, which offered warmth, food, and shelter. There was no other place for me to go, and then the ordeal began. When I walked into the office, not going to the part that housed the passengers, the clerk in worker's uniform sat and stared. I asked for food and told him in Chinese that I was an American. I did not tell him that I was a prisoner.

It was interesting, in a pathetic way, to watch his re-actions, because he did bring me some food before he telephoned someone. Within a short time, a group of Chinese descended upon me with a viciousness that was difficult to comprehend under the circumstances. Three of them jumped upon me, trussed me up so that my head was forced to the floor, and left me bound with my hands tied behind me. I certainly was not a threat to them in any way. One man held a gun on me, and this really irritated me. They were taking the role of those who captured me, assuming that I was a very dangerous prisoner. This was hardly the case. They forced me to lie down near a stove, and weariness overcame me. The heat and the warmth gave me a feeling of security and comfort. I still retained the feeling of being the one in control of the situation.

One thing I had insisted upon was that the members of my flight have a plan to cover any emergency that might arise. The emphasis was on the fact that it was better to have a plan that was possibly not accurate for the situation than to have no plan at all. I had a plan for escape, and when that failed, a plan to return. I enjoyed the heat and the warmth and realized that in spite of what was in store, I was alive. A train stopped in front of the station, going north. This was different from the pattern that I had observed.

I was hustled head down into the train and into an empty Pullman coach. Seated in a corner away from a window, the guards still made me hold my head down. After the train began to move north to the city of Mukden, I was taken to a closed private compartment and again made to hold my head down on the table in the compartment. Still tightly bound, every move that I made, no matter how slight, was answered with admonitions from the guards. Finally, after a ride of some minutes, the train pulled up to the station at Mukden. It was the same station that I had arrived at what seemed like eons ago. Hurried out of the train to a waiting jeep covered with a canvas top, I was taken across the large area in front of the station to a sign that indicated that this was the headquarters of the railway authority. Inside the building I waited for a long period of time. The prospect of a domestic Chinese prison awaited me.

A number of Chinese came in, and many telephone calls were made. Then two guards who had been members of the group that had been with me prior to the escape came, and I was led to another vehicle. The thought that went through my mind was that they were going to take me to another prison that had more stringent security measures. I thought of the prison that Ron, Andy, and Lyle had been in. This seemed the only possibility that I was aware of.

The vehicle took a route that led through the same area where I had been before. When it stopped at the prison gates in Mukden, it was a great surprise to me. I thought they were going to take me to the same cell area that I had been in. I even had hopes that it might be near Ron and Lyle or Andy. Going through the doorway, I was ushered past the familiar cell where I had been held before. We stopped at the cell that was close to the latrine. A delegation of the guards met me. They were highly agitated at me for escaping, because I am sure they were made fools of very badly by the fact that the escape had been made after two weeks of work on my part. The indications were there in the cell that I had intended to escape.

Anger, rage, and the basic emotions are easy to determine in any man's language, and it was easy to see that the guards were violently angry with me for showing them up in their laxity.

The Road Back Home

The anger showed up when the man who was head of the guards came in with some handcuffs. I was going to resist, but there were too many, so I held out my hands. He clamped those handcuffs on so tight that pain shot up my arms and the circulation was cut off. He did this with malice, and I could have killed him easily if given the chance. The metal contacted my wristbone and remained there, yet there was an additional click in the handcuffs as they merged with my flesh at the last possible position. I remained handcuffed in the cell, with the guards looking in the door and enjoying it.

After a few hours, I was taken to the cell that was to remain my home for the next months and where a difficult period of transition happened. The cell was down the hall from my original cell and on the other side of the building. Here there were no walls or windows to the outside and here, too, there was a guard assigned to watch over me. When I arrived at the cell, there again was only a bed and a mattress. I began to throw up because of the dirt and weed stems that I had ingested when I did find some snow for drinking water purposes. Again there was the matter of my feet, which had been frozen when I crossed the river. They began to throb from the unaccustomed heat.

On top of this, the guards would not let me lie down without interruptions. When I had apparently gone to sleep, they would hit the door and wake me up. Finally I could stand this no longer, and I hit the door with all my might. It did not give. Immediately there were a great number of guards who came to the door, disturbed from their sleep. They ranted and raved until I quieted down. I talked to them and explained that the guard was hitting the door. After this they left, and the guard no longer hit the door. He was one of those insipid guards who would have been disliked anywhere—a typical sneaky, underhanded individual who got his kicks out of making life miserable for the prisoners. If the prisoners had killed anyone it would have been this man.

It was impossible to rest. I was sick, my feet hurt, I was vomiting, and the mental environment was the worst. The fact that the handcuffs were on my hands prevented me from sleeping. They were on so tight that the pain was excruciating. The bands caused my wrists to swell so that there was no circulation in my hands. This caused them to throb and ache.

After breakfast the next morning, our old friend Chong came into the room. I believe he was actually hurt that I had escaped and that he had been taken in so effectively. He loosened my handcuffs, so that my blood could circulate. I was grateful to him for this. I thought the handcuffs were to come off entirely, but they were only loosened.

Then began two weeks of difficult living. I was handcuffed the entire time, which made me think about every effort that I made to move my hands. No longer could they be used singly, but had to move as a pair.

At night when I fell asleep and inadvertently jerked my hands, it would wake me up. I slept with literally one eye open, since I was restricted to the movements that I could make in this fashion. This also meant that the clothes I had on must remain on, and it was almost impossible to wash with the meager facilities that were available. For a fortnight these conditions remained the same. That must have been the time that they decreed I had to wear the handcuffs. The moment I was waiting for finally became a reality. The interpreter came in, and with a show of ceremony, a key was produced and the handcuffs came off. It was little things like that that made the future bright. This was one of the favorite Chinese statements: "You have a bright future."

Life developed into a deadly monotony. Then little things began to change. I was able to get books in quantity, and I began to read for eight hours or more a day. Reading became a passion and also a lifesaver. Without reading, surely it would have been easy to go mad. The light in the cell was one small bulb, which must have been, at the maximum, a twenty-five-watt bulb. It burned continuously, and it was a major catastrophe when it burned out. It was a wonder that my eyes held out, but when needed our physical weaknesses are ofttimes overcome by our mental needs. So for hours I would pore over books, and when I could not get anything to read, I asked for books that I had read and reread them, and so it went for months. A new interpreter brought the books, and he was called "Happy Hank." Both he and Chong would visit me, and the topic of conversation was political and social. It seemed a new era was dawning.

Gradually, little by little, the living conditions improved as well as the food. It seemed the improvements were in pace with the meager news that we would get concerning the political situation. The realization that I was not a prisoner of war but a political prisoner dawned gradually, and the feeling that this engendered was not entirely to my liking. It was a difficult situation to be in, between two nations, each dedicated to the eventual demise of the other. What compounded this difficulty of the prisoners was the fact that there were no diplomatic relations between the countries, and no one was acting as the go-between for these two world giants.

In fact, the United States could use us as the living proof of the perfidy of the Chinese Communists, and the Chinese could use us as the living proof of the perfidy of the United States. Never having liked being the middle man, I suddenly found myself with the rest of the prisoners at the center of a huge controversy of international implications. Through analyzing the news of the Communists' English-language newspaper *Hsin Hui,* I was able to understand what our side was saying. The fact that there was no agreement between the two sides was the most discouraging fact of all.

It became readily apparent that the Chinese would not be deterred by the threats of force that the United States gave vent to, but it was also apparent that our continued existence in China could act as a deterrent to them as far as public opinion was concerned. And the Communists were concerned about public opinion.

Spring came and with it a further extension of the lenient policy of the Chinese Red army as it concerned prisoners of war or political prisoners under detention. It was in March of 1954, and I was again taken out of my cell and brought before another group of high-ranking personnel. This was a repeat of the first performance and almost as impressive as the first time when Ron, Lyle, and I were brought together. Only in this case, the fourth individual was with us, and he was Andrew Mackenzie, the lone Canadian flyer with the United Nations forces. The reunion was joyful, and many events had to be covered, since we had been in contact last.

Andy, since he had been absent from us for so long,

was queried the most. Again it was a marathon of talking, with everyone attempting to talk at once and
hardly anyone listening. In the evening after bedtime,
the conversation was analyzed and thought about. This
was the time also when it was not difficult for me to
face a new day, because there was someone to talk to
and to answer back. It was a world of new ideas that in-
trigued my cohorts and me. The idea of world domina-
tion by communism was discussed; we used to think
that the place was "bugged," so our ideas were carefully phrased. When we did disagree with the accepted
party line, which we all knew at this time, it was in
carefully modulated tones and in as isolated an area as
possible.

There were many changes in the old cell block, and
it did not seem possible that this was the same area we
had entered long ago. All the doors were taken off the
cells, and we converted one cell into a dining room, another for sleeping, another for the library, and a cell for
the game or music room. The guards were no longer
merely to keep us in our rooms but to assist us if we
needed anything. Many of the old guards who had been
with us in the beginning resisted this tremendously.

The library consisted now of over two hundred vol-
umes of the world's classics, and if I were ever a prisoner again, I'd want it to be in a library. Here I was
able to read some of the great works of literature that
would be impossible to read at any other time or place.
The library was enjoyed by all of us, and I systematically attempted to go through every book from
Thorsten Veblen's *Theory of the Leisure Class* to Tol-
stoy's *Anna Karenina*. If there was a good side to being
a prisoner, this was it.

Music, in which I had always had an interest, became an avocation under these circumstances. Lyle had at one time been an accordion instructor, and the Chinese furnished us with a violin and an accordion. All of us immediately attempted to play the accordion under Lyle's instructions. When Lyle picked up the instrument and played the old favorites, such as "Body and Soul" and "Stardust," it was a taste of home that was at times bitter under the circumstances.

A Ping-Pong table was available to the prisoners, and millions of games were played on the table. Chess and bridge occupied a great deal of our time. So, all in all, the time was not entirely wasted when you could apply yourself to the various pursuits that were available to the prisoners.

An event that we all looked forward to at this time was writing and receiving mail from home through the Red Cross of China. Those first letters were so carefully edited and written that they were almost masterpieces. They were calculated to impress the public and friends in the States with the lenient attitude of the Chinese.

Since our letters were censored both coming in and going out, we were kept in a somewhat sterile atmosphere as to what those who were sending these letters really felt, and we had to be careful. If we wrote what the conditions had been or anything slightly derogatory about the Chinese or their government, it would be impossible to have a letter sent. Therefore, our letters were full of cheerfulness and hope and a somewhat accurate indication of exactly what our living conditions were. But there were still ways to indicate that things were not as rosy as depicted, since it was apparently easy to show that what we were putting in our letters was not the way things were. My father did not like chocolate malted milk, and when I wrote that I was reminiscing about how he did like it, it was a clue that everything was not as it should be.

Under these circumstances life was tolerable, even being a prisoner. One of the things that the prisoners enjoyed the most was the bath that we were allowed to have once every two weeks. It was pure luxury to go to the bathhouse, which all the guards used, and to soak in the hot water. I still carry a scar on my behind from when I backed up against a radiator just prior to entering the concrete bath tub.

However good the circumstances, there were instances when there were personality conflicts within the group. One member of the four of us had a tendency to be selfish, which was magnified under the circumstances. Another was unable to accept defeat in anything he attempted. I was an egotist, and another was stubborn. These personality defects erupted in violence one evening, and serious physical damage was prevented by the guards coming in and breaking it up. It was not anyone's fault, and it is impossible to change the habits of a lifetime, which were only accentuated by prison life.

It would soon be two years since I had bailed out of the F-86. The events in the prison went along tranquilly. And then it happened: Andy Mackenzie was called in one day and told that he was going home. This was the greatest news that we could get other than that we could go home ourselves. Sincerely, all of us enjoyed the moment as much as Andy did. Not without a trace of sadness we watched him go out the door. However, all of us sent our best wishes with him.

Another prisoner that we were aware of now came into focus. Many times I had mentioned Ed Heller and wondered how he was. And many times during the stay, one interpreter or another had mentioned that Ed Heller was coming along well. They mentioned that he had been wounded and that it had taken him a long time to recover, but this was all that we really knew about Ed Heller and his life. The three of us knew that books were being taken to another prisoner, and we decided to place a message in one of the books between the lines for Ed, telling him about us and where we were.

When this book was returned a few days later, we hastily looked through it for an answer to our message. Sure enough, these books had been going to Ed Heller, who was in an area that was not very far away from where we were, evidently in the same building. It was good to have contact with Ed, and we all looked forward to seeing him. We began a concentrated effort to have Ed join us, and our suggestions, which the Chinese encouraged us to make, were listened to.

Without a great deal of fanfare, there came a gaunt figure across the threshold of our cells. Preceding this, there had been a concerted interrogation of both Ron and me concerning the border violations of the 51st FIW [Fighter-Intercept Wing]. The Chinese were building up a mass of evidence, both false and partly true, concerning Ed's case. It was finally being settled so that he could join us. When he came across the threshold, he was gray and walked with a noticeable limp. He was one of those that I had known before and had admired. He dared to defy the ritual of the military when he deemed that it would be desirable—in other words, he was a free thinker.

He was an ace from World War II, and he would have been one again if he had not been shot down. He was a flyer who loved to fly—one of the old school, where flying was everything. There was much in the man that one could admire, and while being so strong in some respects, he also had his share of weaknesses, as all of us do.

He brought the total of aces to three in the group—Andy, the Canadian ace, Ed Heller, and myself. The three of us had destroyed over twenty enemy aircraft that had threatened our respective countries in two wars, and now we had been added to the list of pilots on the other side. Two of us were there because we made our own rules, as did a lot of others, but Andy was there because he was just unlucky. The three of us were different from the population in general, because we had been better than average in our profession.

Events began to transpire that indicated to us that there might possibly be a chance for us to go home. This was evidenced by better living conditions and food. And never did prisoners enjoy the food more. It was rich and as Americanized for us as possible. One of the things that we had asked for was a trip to actually see how it was in new China. Remarkably enough, it was granted. We were allowed to go to the park for a day. The park was in the northern part of the city of Mukden, and the American truck that took us out to the park was canvas covered with an open end. It was a minimum-security situation, and being free for the second time for almost two years was a tremendous emotional experience for all of us.

When we returned to the prison area, we were treated to a movie, which now had become a weekly affair. This was almost too much excitement for the average prisoner, and we dropped into bed dead tired. If we were to be released soon, this was a very good way for our captors to treat us. Bad memories are often repressed and the most recent good memories have a tendency to remain. Also it is difficult to condemn that which should be condemned with good conscience, if the recent memories are good. There is much to be said for the axiom that the Chinese are master psychologists.

Questions and actions led me to believe that I was going or that we were going to be released after I had been in prison for two years or so on the seventh of April. Chong made many veiled suggestions to me and to the others, and after being with the man two years, I began to feel that I had at least begun to understand and evaluate what he would say and what it would mean. Many indications led up to this feeling: the Red Cross packages from home were arriving sometimes before we could complete the ones that we had; mail was coming and going as fast as possible; and our food from the Chinese was excellent. It was interesting to note that whenever we did receive food parcels from home, it would be after an exceptionally good meal, so that the delicacies from home would not leave such a good impression on us. But the seventh of April came and went, and nothing happened. Life again returned to normal. The season changed, and it was spring again in China.

Life went on after the big disappointment. We had thought that after the secretary general of the United Nations had visited China, supposedly on behalf of the prisoners who were held in China, that there might be a chance for our release. The secretary general visited China in January, and there had been a flurry of activity at that time that included physicals, dental treatment, and a flood of mail. The initial mail that I had received included letters written from my mother that had been held up for months. She had written every day, so I had received a great deal of mail.

It was interesting for us to sit down and read our mail. We would go into the library, and after each of us had read it privately, we would read it out loud for all of us to hear. This way each of us could enjoy the mail four times over, and we got to know just about everything that a letter could reveal. This was also the time that Andy was arriving home to a hero's welcome and, true to his promise that he would visit each of our parents, he traveled from Canada down to Iowa and Nebraska and talked to all our parents, which they enjoyed because they were learning about their sons. But they also enjoyed the publicity.

Then late in May there was another flurry of excitement, and Chong came in one day to ask us to pack our clothes. The air was tense with excitement, as we all thought this might be it—the day we were waiting for. I had been prepared for this for a long time and had written a partial book, which I had secreted in the lining of my sweatshirt. But prior to departure, it was found. After thinking he was going to find something, Chong disgustedly gave up and stated that there was nothing in the book. For a long period of time, while he was going through the book, which was written in fine print, he looked as if he had been through a great deal. His eyes were bloodshot and he looked as if he had been on a long weekend. But the upshot of it all was that what I had written was drivel or trash and had no political content at all. And life went on.

Gathering our few belongings, we were escorted again to the train station and placed on a train. They would not tell us where we were going, but from the direction and the terrain with which we were now familiar, we guessed that we were going through Tientsin. All along the route, we could see the pillboxes that the Japanese had constructed along main rail lines to protect their trains, and then the Kuomintang had taken them over. Now they were abandoned. The trip was one that was undertaken with a great deal of abandon and happiness, for any change was exciting, and we knew that soon we would be free. All the indications were that we would be.

The train pulled into the station at Peking, which was the showplace and the capital. As we were nearing the station, I saw manned gun emplacements on the wall surrounding the city, which were probably antiaircraft guns. Also in view was the wonder of the world, the Great Wall. We questioned where we would be taken, and it was not long before we found out. A taxi of sorts took us to an area in the center of Peking, an old ancestral home.

It had evidently been owned by a wealthy Chinese family. There were three buildings—one for the family or the head of the family, one for the children when they married, and one for the servants. The home for the servants included the kitchen and the latrine, which was used by all. Around the entire area was a large wall, which was the custom with this type of housing. The four of us occupied the area that the head of the household had occupied. There was a large room with many windows facing the south to heat the dwelling.

Now the food parcels really began arriving, and also the mail. We began to get mail from all over the United States, and the publicity grew with our imprisonment in Peking. Food parcels and the good food that we were now eating had an effect on us. When we had very little to eat, our thoughts did not include the female sex, but with good food and the stimulation of the letters we were receiving, our thoughts again turned to past times, to the sports that healthy men engage in with the opposite sex.

Another trip was planned for us, and this time it was to one of the great tourist spots of the world before the Communist menace—the Dowager Empress's summer home. She was the empress who reigned in the late 1800s and was famous for signing death warrants. Near her summer home was a large lake where she reviewed the Chinese navy, which had to be transported inland, according to our interpreter. Close to her summer home was a large marble replica of a paddle wheel boat, which had so impressed her at one time that she had one built. She had seven homes constructed in the area. One included her personal shrine, which held an enormous Buddha. Close to this temple were two other small shrines, which held two additional Buddhas.

All this was at the top of a hill that must have been 200 feet high, which had to be reached by the means of steep winding steps. She was carried to the top and to the bottom of the steps daily. It was interesting to see the sights and to smell freedom again, and to see the people that we had read about for over two years. But although the sights were more appealing than the day trip we took at Mukden, they did not have the emotional impact the first visit to the park had. The first visit included photographs that we sent home, and this visit did not. We theorized that there was not enough time to get them developed before we were to go home.

The small, quaint Chinese home that we were living in was only temporary, and we were moved to another area that was part of a large, old school, evidently for the very well-to-do. Here we each had a room and again had that privacy during the evening that we had grown up with and the comradeship during the day. This was the closest to American living that could be achieved. Interrogations continued into every aspect of military life. Now we were interrogated not separately but as a group about the military and governmental affairs of our country.

We were told that we were going to be tried, but that we were also to remember the leniency of the Chinese policy. We were not told the charges, but they stated that we would be given counsel. The thought itself was frightening, but it was indicated that our sentence was already decided, and that we should have nothing to worry about. We all felt that it was a formality that would have to be put up with. However, an active imagination does not rest easy under these circumstances.

We met our duly appointed counsels. Each of us had one from the university. All were supposedly instructors at the University of People's Law. I met mine, and we talked for a few minutes. He asked me how I would plead to violating the sacred territorial air of China. This was not the time to refute my violation, since I had landed in China, so I pleaded guilty and placed myself on the mercy of the court. This was to be my stand and everyone else's.

The day of the trial dawned. We were taken to the main municipal court building in Peking, the capital of the People's Republic of China. There, before a packed audience and before what we were told was the Supreme Court of China, our charges were read, first in Chinese and then in English, and we each stood up and pleaded guilty. After an indeterminable length of time, we were asked again to stand up, and the four of us—Ed on my left, Ron and Lyle on my right—received with a great deal of relief the sentence of the court. It was that "we were to be expelled from the People's Republic of China without delay, and if we were ever to enter China again, we would be duly punished." From the courthouse, we were escorted to a train that was going south. With us was the man who met me when I initially went to Peking, Chong Chung.

We traveled down to the south of China, across the Yellow River by ferry, there being no railroad across this most terrible of rivers, then south to Canton, where we spent the longest days of our internment after the first thirty days of initial captivity. For some reason our delay was necessary to complete the final processing. Again we were taken for an outing as we stayed in an old abandoned army camp. We went to the graves of the Seven Martyrs, which was an imposing park, then through the foreign settlement where the ambassadors and foreign dignitaries lived at one time. This area had been off limits to all Chinese, and it held fine western homes. Surrounding the area was a moat that kept the unwanted away. Now it was a symbol of the new regime, and the homes were turned into workers' apartments. We noticed that around the city there were more armed Chinese soldiers than we had seen anywhere else. Canton was close to the coastal waters and to the protectorate of Hong Kong, where we were to be expelled.

The day arrived, and it was a normal day for millions of people, but for the four of us, it was freedom day; a day that we had longed for, never knowing when it would arrive. We took a train trip without forewarning, as had been the policy during our entire stay, to the environs of Hong Kong. Then there was another delay while we ate with "Hate America" posters on the walls. Finally there was that long trip over a short strip of land after being examined by customs agents. The gates dropped down and shut, and, for a moment, we were in no-man's-land. The first man who greeted us was a Jesuit priest, who said, "Welcome to a free land again."

Nearly forty years later, in April 1994, Fischer traveled to Kiev, Ukraine, to meet former Soviet pilots who flew in Korea. There he met one of his adversaries from the dogfight of April 7, 1953, confirming that he had indeed run up against a Honcho that day.

In November 1997, while visiting Red China, he met General Han Decai, who takes credit for shooting Fischer down. General Decai invited Fischer back to China during President Clinton's 1998 visit, at which time Fischer discussed the development of a Chinese-American Foundation.

16

ENDINGS

Colonel Fischer did not return to America until 1955, but for most pilots the war ended in 1953. It was the death of Stalin that seems to have been the event that finally started the winding down of the conflict that was going nowhere.

By the end of 1952, there were clear indications that China increasingly wanted out of the conflict as much as America did. Like the Americans, China entered the conflict first with the intention of preventing the collapse of its client state, and then with the far broader goal of eliminating the client of its enemy. By the end of the "Big Red Attack" offensive of mid-1951, it was already apparent to the Chinese that a purely military solution was no longer possible. Next they had opted for a political wearing down.

The election of Eisenhower in 1952 ended that as well. Though Ike had been vague with his campaign promises of having a war-winning solution, after his inauguration the pressure started to notch up.

After the stabilization of the front in 1951, United

Nations strategy had been one of maintaining air superiority of North Korea and then of inflicting staggering punishment from above. Though there is
debate to this day as to the effectiveness of any strategic air campaign not backed up by ground assault, it is
clear that the damage delivered to the Chinese and
Koreans was brutal.

In Ike's first State of the Union address on February
2, 1953, the president declared that the mission of the
Seventh Fleet, patrolling the Formosa Strait, would no
longer be that of a peacekeeping force preventing
hostilities between the Reds and the Nationalists. In
the future, if the Nationalists wanted to launch strikes
against the mainland, the Seventh Fleet would make
no move to stop them. The implication was clear as
well that if China should attempt to strike back, however, the Seventh would be unleashed to counterattack.

Economically, the war was proving to be a tremendous drain on Red China at a time when Mao was still
working to consolidate his political hold on the country. Though Korea had served as a useful campaign in
the early days, a cause to rally nationalistic support to
the Reds, after two years it was proving to be as much
an albatross around the necks of the Reds as it was
around that of the United Nations.

The Soviets, however, were more than content to let
the struggle continue. Korea was tying down hundreds of thousands of American troops, consuming
vast quantities of supplies, and proving to be a wonderful diversion from the far more crucial European
situation. As long as it did not serve as a trigger to a
global conflict, Stalin was content to let the fight go on

forever. It is evident as well that though Stalin was more than delighted to have China go Red, it was another thing altogether fully to trust Russia's ancient enemy in East Asia. If Korea should serve to drain off not only American but also Red Chinese military and economic strength, so much the better.

Fortunately for the entire world, Stalin finally was removed from our presence on March 5, 1953.

Within weeks the Chinese were signaling a clear desire to wrap up the conflict. At Stalin's funeral the new Soviet boss, Georgy Malenkov, made an open statement about the need for peaceful competition between the Communist and non-Communist world.

On March 30, 1953, a major break came when the Chinese backed down on their hard-line stance regarding the return of all prisoners to their home territories, a major sticking point, since thousands of Chinese and North Korean POWs had openly defected to our side and if forced to return, would have undoubtedly faced execution. The betrayal of millions of Russian POWs and civilians back into Soviet hands at Yalta still lingered, and the United States, in a remarkable display of idealism, stood firm on the rights of former enemy soldiers who had renounced their masters and wanted to stay free.

By early April, at the same time that Colonel Fischer went up for his last mission, details were hammered out regarding the immediate release of sick and wounded prisoners prior to a final armistice agreement. But after the exchange of these personnel ended early in May, the negotiations again slowed down over the issue of forced repatriation.

Throughout the last eighteen months of the war it had been the air forces' dirty task to apply maximum pressure against the Reds, and though peace seemed but a single negotiating session away, FEAF aircraft were again unleashed to exert influence on the enemy.

If ever there was a true display of professionalism on the part of air force and navy pilots it was in these last three months. It was quite literally possible that a pilot could take off on a mission, lose his life, and have his comrades return home, and an hour later receive the news that an agreement had been reached and the war was over, the last death having had no influence whatsoever on the outcome.

If anything, these final days were an opportunity for the true Hot Shots to prove themselves. Thirty-two MiGs were dropped in the last month of the war. On July 15, 1953, Major James Jabara made his fifteenth kill, placing him one behind Captain J. D. McConnell as the leading jet ace of the war. On July 22, Lieutenant Sam Young, of the 51st Wing nailed his first MiG, which also was the last one shot down in the Korean War.

For the next three days, bad weather kept both MiGs and Sabres grounded. Thanks in large part to the unrelenting pressure from the air, the Chinese agreed to significantly scale back their demands.

On July 27, an armistice was announced. In the closing hours, the Sabres went up for one more sweep along MiG Alley, but the Chinese and North Korean air forces remained on the ground or on the other side of the Yalu.

Captain Ralph Parr, on one final patrol, spotted an IL-12 transport, an unfamiliar sight in the air over Korea. Sweeping in to make sure of his target, he spotted the red stars on the wings, swung in behind his target, and dropped it. This was the final Hot Shot kill of the

Korean War, and with it Parr graduated to the rank of double ace.

Three hours later the Korean War was over.

It had been a war of over a million sorties, at times rivaling in intensity the bloody conflict over the skies of Europe in late 1944 and early 1945. Over 700,000 sorties were flown by FEAF, and more than 100,000 by marine air units. Non-American air units flew just under 50,000 missions, and the United States Navy took it over the million mark with nearly 170,000 missions.

Over 700,000 tons of ordnance were dropped, including more than 30,000 tons of napalm, and well over 100 million rounds of machine gun ammunition was expended.

The damage inflicted in this limited war on a small peninsula was staggering. The records show that nearly 1,000 locomotives, 10,000 railroad cars, over 80,000 vehicles, nearly 600 boats, 65 tunnels, more than 1,000 bridges, and 100,000 buildings were destroyed.

As for the damage to one's fellow man, it is estimated that nearly 200,000 enemy troops were killed by air strikes. The number of wounded is unknown, but given even a conservative estimate, based upon the standard ratio of dead to wounded in combat, the figure could well approach half a million. Total enemy losses therefore would have exceeded the total number of troops in several dozen divisions.

Airpower alone most certainly did not win the unwinnable war, but it most certainly went a long way toward preventing defeat and forcing the enemy to the negotiating table. Without clear air superiority, the cost of American lives in that conflict would have been staggering, perhaps even approaching the number of men lost in World War II.

Airpower slowed the initial offensive of 1950 and helped to stabilize the front around the Pusan pocket. It most definitely played a role in severely punishing the North Koreans during their headlong retreat after Inchon. Without a doubt it saved the lives of tens of thousands of American and allied troops during the winter debacle of 1950–1951, and was a major factor in the collapse of the Chinese offensive at the 38th parallel. During the spring it severely hampered the buildup for the "Big Red Attack" offensive, and when that attack was launched, air strikes slaughtered tens of thousands of enemy troops.

Throughout the long months of negotiation the continued air strikes exacted a terrible price on Red China for its continued aggression. The Hot Shot units flying Sabres along the Yalu faced down odds exceeding those encountered by the RAF during the Battle of Britain.

Official air force records indicate a total of 976 enemy aircraft destroyed by all units engaged in the conflict. United Nations losses were just under 2,000 aircraft, of which nearly half were lost due to nonenemy action, such as pilot error, mechanical failure, and accidents. Most losses were credited to flak, while only 147 aircraft were shot down in air-to-air encounters.

Thus the final kill ratio was nearly seven to one, a remarkable record given the odds that were faced on a daily basis in MiG Alley. This record, more than any other statistic, tells us just how remarkable the Hot Shots truly were and clearly backs up General Risner's reply to the Honcho that if they had ever met, the Honcho would never have come back alive.

It was an unwinnable war, a holding action in the long twilight struggle of half a century. It was a transition from the total victory of World War II to the total disaster of Vietnam. Tragically many of the lessons learned in Korea were forgotten in little more than ten years. As Colonel Blesse pointed out so angrily, the gun was still a key ingredient to victory in air-to-air combat, yet aircraft being deployed to Vietnam only a decade later carried only rockets.

Safe havens existed again, this time in spades as significant portions of North Vietnam were declared off limits. Rather than thirty-five men disappearing, it is clear that hundreds of pilots, including more than one who had survived the skies of North Korea, were abandoned in the name of a so-called peace treaty, and left to die in the hands of their Vietnamese, Chinese and, perhaps, even Soviet captors.

The final price for Korea was 1,144 air force personnel killed in air combat, and an additional 36 dead in ground actions. Thirty-five men, known to be alive, were still in enemy hands a year after the end of the war. Several, such as Colonel Fischer, eventually returned home; the others disappeared, many of them into the Soviet gulag.

May their sacrifice not be in vain.